D0170707

Complete Cornwall

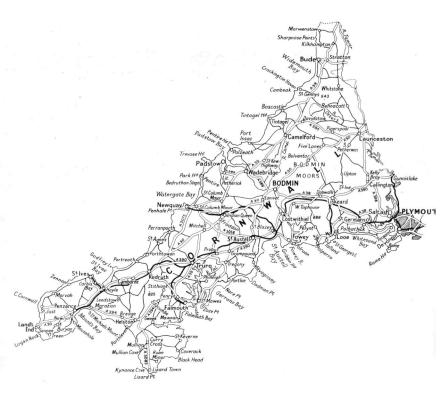

RED GUIDE

Complete **Cornwall**

Reginald J. W. Hammond, F.R.G.S.
and
Kenneth E. Lowther, M.A.

WARD LOCK LIMITED
LONDON

© Ward Lock Limited 1977

ISBN 0 7063 5355 2

First published in Great Britain in 1977
by Ward Lock Limited, 116 Baker Street,
London, WIM 2BB, a member of the Pentos
Group.

All Rights Reserved. No part of this publication
may be reproduced, stored in a retrieval system, or
transmitted, in any form or by any means,
electronic, mechanical, photocopying, recording, or
otherwise, without the prior permission of the
copyright owner.

Photographs by Peter Baker
and Tony Kersting

Plans based upon the Ordnance Survey map with the
sanction of the Controller of HM Stationery Office

Text filmset in Plantin

Printed and bound by
Butler & Tanner Ltd
Frome and London

Contents

Maps and Plans

Illustrations

Introduction

A Land of Legend

To visit Cornwall is to travel beyond the bounds of the commonplace, into practically another country. It is often forgotten that Cornwall is almost an island, that from its eastern limit at Plymouth Sound right up to its north-eastern border runs the wide-sweeping River Tamar, cutting it off from the rest of England. On the map the isolation may seem imaginary, yet Cornwall is quite distinct from the rest of England. Its people and customs are different, and for centuries it spoke a language all its own, half-brother to the Welsh and Breton tongues.

Well before St Augustine came to England the Christian faith had taken root in this western peninsula, and ancient relics may still be seen by the wayside of the Irish and Breton pilgrims who wandered through the county and won its people over to Christianity. West of Penzance one searches in vain for a reference to any saint mentioned in standard hagiology. The Cornish character for independence asserted itself even in this matter. St Levan, St Buryan, St Sennen, St Just, St Piran, St Uny and St Elwyn are the names of just a few of the saints to whom churches round Land's End are dedicated.

But there are more ancient memorials than the names of churches. There are relics dating from times when fact and tradition are inextricably intermingled. There are the thrilling tales of King Arthur and his knights, of which Tennyson tells us (and it is interesting to know that every place mentioned in the story of Tristan and Isolde has been identified in Cornwall). There are the fabulous stories of Lyonnesse, that fair land with its one hundred and forty churches which was buried beneath the sea and now lies at the bottom between Land's End and the Scilly Isles; and there are the cromlechs, rocking-stones and other witnesses to the early residents of the peninsula.

Cornwall attracts vast numbers of holiday makers with its magnificent rocky headlands, its sandy coves and beaches, its breezy moorland tracks. The man-made attractions of the orthodox seaside resort pall somewhat when compared with the brilliant colours of the water, the scenic grandeur of towering cliffs and the natural beauty of the sandy porths which breach them at frequent intervals. On the north coast the surging Atlantic is kept at bay by the finest stretch of cliff scenery in the British Isles. The south coast offers the less rugged and more restful charms of sheltered coves, wooded estuaries and quaint fishing villages.

Getting Around
By Road
There are few parts of Britain more popular with motorists than Cornwall, for a great proportion of it is well beyond the reach of the railway and a car is almost essential to a holiday unless one is an enthusiastic walker or is content to remain in one place.

The road system depends upon the main east–west highway running by Liskeard, Lostwithiel, St Austell, Truro and Helston to the Land's End. It is an ancient road, laid out in the days when deep inlets of the sea had to be skirted and so it touches the head of the Looe River, the Fowey River, St Austell Bay, the Fal and Helford River, and down each of the combes run subsidiary roads serving the towns at their lower ends. These are the main roads—all good, with smooth safe, surfaces, and with a widely varied beauty; but in addition there are a number of smaller lanes which climb the intervening hills and link up the large number of hamlets and villages which provide holiday quarters for so many motorists each summer.

Long-distance coaches run to the main resorts from London and large provincial centres. Within the county Western National buses operate a wide network of services.

By Rail
The famous Cornish Riviera main line to Penzance still provides magnificent views for railway travellers, but local services have been drastically curtailed in recent years. Only four branch lines survive—Truro to Falmouth, Par to Newquay, St Erth to St Ives and Liskeard to Looe. In addition motorail services operate in the season between Penzance and London and between St Austell and London, Crewe, Reading and Worcester.

Youth Hostels in Cornwall
Youth Hostels are intended for those who are moving from place to place, and not more than three consecutive nights may generally be spent at the same hostel. All hostel users must be members of a recognized

Youth Hostels Association and must take a sheet sleeping bag or hire one at the hostel. Meals are, in nearly all cases, provided at the hostels and there are always cooking facilities for those who wish to cook for themselves. For further information apply to National Office, Trevelyan House, 8 St Stephen's Hill, St Albans, Herts.

Youth Hostels in the Area
Penquite House, Golant, Fowey.
Riviere House, 20 Parc-An-Dix Lane, Phillack, Hayle.
Letcha Vean, St Just-in-Penwith, Penzance.
Pendennis Castle, Falmouth.
Castle Horneck, Alverton, Penzance.
Dunderhole Point, Tintagel.
Tregonnan, Treyarnon, Padstow.

Bude

Bathing From the beach at the foot of the sand-hills under Summerleaze Downs, Crooklets, and at Maer Lake Cove, at the northern end of the town. Huts may be hired. The tide goes a long way out and bathing from the sands at *low water* or on an ebb tide needs extreme caution. The fine breakers provide marvellous surf-bathing.

The excellent and extensive Bathing Pool and the smaller and more primitive Sir Thomas's Pit, among the rocks at the end of the Breakwater, make it possible to bathe in safety and comfort at all times.

Bowls At the Bude Haven Recreation Ground.

Buses To Boscastle and Camelford; to Bideford (via Kilkhampton, Hartland and Clovelly); to Holsworthy and Torrington etc.; to Poughill, Marhamchurch and Widemouth; to Launceston and Plymouth; to Wadebridge and Newquay.

Cinema Bude Picture House, Summerleaze Down.

Distances Barnstaple, 35 miles; Bodmin, 30; Boscastle, 15; Clovelly, 18; Exeter, 50; London, 220; Newquay, 46; Tintagel, 19.

Early Closing Thursday.

Fishing Bass etc. can be caught from the Breakwater and rocks. The Canal is well stocked with coarse fish.

Golf Bude and North Cornwall Club on Summerleaze Down.

Hotels *Burn Court; Ceres; Chough*, Upton; *Falcon; Flexbury Lodge; Grenville; Grosvenor; Hartland; Hotel Meva-Gwin*, Upton; *Maer Lodge; Mornish; Penarvor; Penwethers*.

Library The Castle.

Population 4,069.

Squash Bude Haven.

Tennis Bude Haven, Summerleaze Down, the Sports Ground at Stratton.

Bude is laid out on the southern slopes of a broad tongue of rising land almost filling a mile-wide gap in the rocky wall that Cornwall presents to the Atlantic. There is no formal front at Bude, the 'Parade' is a broad stretch of open turf bounded on the west and south by low cliffs below which are wonderful expanses of firm golden sand. If one part of the town more than another resembles a promenade it is the **Strand,** part of the business thoroughfare, bounded on one side by shops, hotels and banks, and on the other by the picturesque *River Neet.* Although a busy little town, it is almost surrounded by open downland; and though a seaside resort it overlooks two fresh-water channels. Bathing and surfing, tennis, golf, bowls, cricket, rowing, riding, hunting—practically every sport is followed with zest, and the wide grass-covered expanse, known as **Summerleaze Downs,** with the glorious sands, form an ideal playground for children.

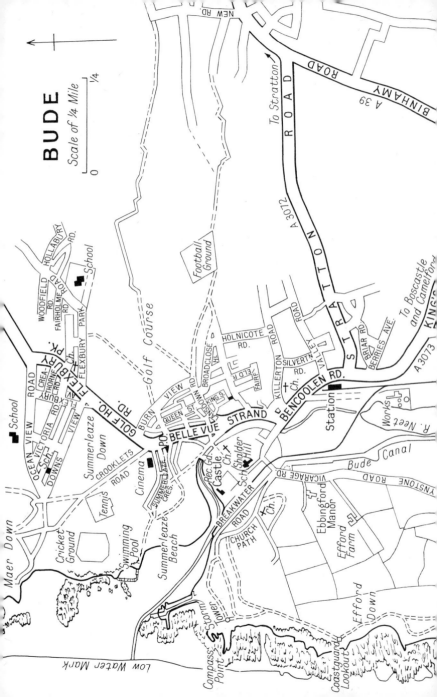

Opposite the Strand and across the river is a large tract of land, which the Canal on the farther side almost makes an island, broken by a high tussocky mound known as the **Shalder Hill.** On top, in a conspicuous position, is the **War Memorial,** overlooking the **Methodist Church,** and the **Drill Hall,** and on the flat ground seaward is the **Recreation Ground,** with tennis courts and bowling and putting greens and a pavilion in which table tennis and squash are played. At the seaward end of this tract, sheltered by huge grassy banks, stands the **Castle** (municipal offices), built by Sir Goldsworthy Gurney, the Cornish engineer, inventor of the steam blow-pipe and of one of the earliest steam road-locomotives.

Ebbingford Manor (*end of May to mid-September, Tuesday, Wednesday and Thursday, also Sundays July to September*) is a typical Cornish manor house dating from the twelfth century, with a walled garden.

The river is spanned by two bridges, one a modern concrete structure on the Stratton road, the other an ancient device of stone and wood, known as **Nanny Moore's Bridge.** A mill stood here of old, and it is suggested that the wooden span at the western end of the bridge marks the place occupied by the wheel.

The Bude and Holsworthy Canal built in 1826 and now only navigable for little more than a mile connects with the sea by means of a lock, the gates of which serve as a footbridge leading to Compass Hill and the Downs.

Bude Haven is a small bay opening to the sea at the mouth of the river.

Bathing in the open sea at Bude is safe except at low water when it is best to use the excellent **Bathing Pool,** at the foot of the cliffs under Summerleaze Down. The pool is one acre in extent, with graduated depths and changing tents.

For children there is Sir Thomas's Pit near Chapel Rock. At spring tides the water at Bude rises 23 feet, at neap 17 feet, which is higher than at any other place in Cornwall. With a strong wind the sea at spring flood is a marvellous sight, and the pounding of the waves can be heard many miles inland.

The Breakwater, reached by a path at the end of Breakwater Road, close to the lock gates, protects the Canal entrance and also serves as a promenade. Its irregular stones are certainly unconventional, but the structure affords a means of getting into close contact with the sea, and is a sheltered spot for writing or reading.

The rock with flagstaff at the end of the Breakwater is called **Chapel**

Rock, from a chapel once standing here. The flagstaff was erected to assist the passage of vessels in and out of the little harbour, though there is practically no shipping at Bude these days.

The extensive **Sands** are firm and dry at lower water, and are among the finest on the coast.

The fine expanse of grassland separating the two parts of the town is called **Summerleaze.** Situated here are the golf links and, adjoining them, tennis courts and a cricket ground. The grassy slopes on the southern and western sides of Summerleaze, with seats and shelter and a café below, form a pleasant promenade.

On the Breakwater side of the Haven a few steps lead up to a gate giving access to a path to the Breakwater and **Compass Point,** from which there is a magnificent view. On the summit is a storm tower, its sides indicating the points of the compass.

Southward to Widemouth extend the delightful **Efford Downs. Efford Beacon** is the highest point and is the site of a coastguard station. To the north tier upon tier of rugged headlands may be seen: Maer High Cliff, Sandymouth, Morwenstow Look-out, Hennacliff and Sharpnose. South-west there is an even grander view. Trevose Head lies low on the horizon, followed by Pentire Point, Tintagel, Boscastle, Crackington, Millook and Widemouth Bay.

Excursions from Bude

1. To Poughill, Combe Valley, Morwenstow and Kilkhampton
Follow the road to the north through Flexbury and turn right for the pretty village of **Poughill** (pronounced *Poffil*). The foundation of the church is Norman and the bowl of the font beside the south door is of the Norman–Transitional period. The main building and tower date from the late fourteenth century. The wall paintings showing St Christopher were repainted in 1894. The carved bench-ends display emblems of the Crucifixion.

Turn left about ½ mile beyond the church and left again at Stibb about 2 miles further on. The road down into **Combe Valley** is steep (1 in 7) and winding but the woods are delightful. The valley is a vast depression, with steep hills, thickly wooded, and with a stream flowing out to sea. A good point from which to see the valley is about ½ mile inland, where it divides, giving a beautiful double view. Another lovely scene—

the meeting of the valleys by the mill and on towards the sea—is opened up along the steep road to Morwenstow. The picturesque mill is set in the midst of semi-tropical vegetation and from the little bridge ferns and flowers may be seen mirrored in the pools. There is a car park at the mill and a road right down to the beach which has good sands.

Cross the stream and ascend the steep farther side of the combe. In a little over 2 miles turn left at cross-roads to reach the Green, where stand the *Bush Inn*, tea gardens and a few cottages. At the far end of the Green turn to the right and Morwenstow church soon comes into sight. About midway between Combe Valley and Morwenstow is **Stanbury Mouth** which has a sandy beach.

Morwenstow lies in a secluded combe on the coast. Church and house stand alone with no other building in sight but the adjacent farm. This place achieved fame through that learned but eccentric poet Robert Stephen Hawker who was vicar from 1834 to 1875. The church is one of the most interesting in the county. The entrance door to the nave is of fine Norman work with zigzag moulding. It was defaced by the removal of the outer of the three orders to form the arch of the sixteenth-century porch. Note the heads projecting in the spandrels of the

Morwenstow Church, from the south

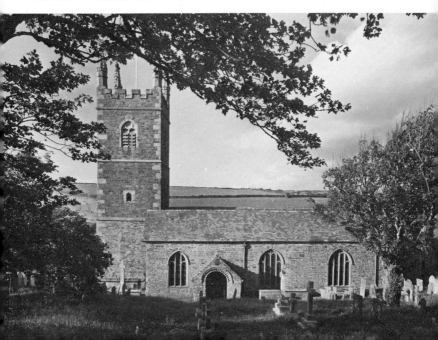

arches. The font is irregular and ornamented with a roughly tooled cable pattern. The screen incorporates some of the original work of 1575. There are the remains of a wall painting on the north chancel wall. The chimney stacks of the nearby vicarage, built by Hawker, represent the towers of churches with which he had been connected.

About 2 miles north of Morwenstow and best reached by the glorious cliff walk is **Marsland Mouth,** a beautiful combe which, with its stream over 400 feet below the surrounding hills, divides Cornwall from Devon.

From Morwenstow follow the road south-east through Woodford to **Kilkhampton** (*London Inn*). The village is situated nearly 600 feet above sea level and the tall tower of the church is conspicuous over a wide area. The building is mainly Perpendicular with some striking remains of Norman work. On the porch are the arms of John Granville, Rector, with the date 1567 and the words 'Porta Celi'. This is the date of the rebuilding of the porch. The church itself was rebuilt in the late fifteenth or early sixteenth century. The south doorway is a rich example of late Norman work with zigzag ornamentation and heads similar to the porch at Morwenstow. Every bench-end is carved in oak black with age, the subjects being emblems of the Passion, initials and a few grotesques. The decoration of the roofs especially in the chancel is extremely beautiful.

The return to Bude is by the A39.

II. To Stratton and Launcells

Stratton is a quiet little town about 2 miles inland from Bude, set in a hollow among hills. It contains many lovely old houses but the outstanding feature is the church. This contains good examples of Norman work, some fine carvings and a wagon roof. Here is the tomb of Sir John Arundell (died 1561) with brasses showing him, his two wives, seven daughters and three sons. Sir John was Vice-Admiral of the West to Henry VIII and was knighted at the Battle of the Spurs. Note the Norman font and the curious poor-box, dated 1707, on the belfry steps. On a window-sill in the north aisle are the old stocks, and on another sill a damaged effigy of a knight.

The **Tree Inn** was formerly the manor house of the Grenvilles. On a wall is a tablet recalling the Battle of Stamford which took place in 1643 a mile north-west of Stratton.

Follow the road skirting the south side of the churchyard. In about 1½ miles turn right and shortly a by-lane on the right leads to **Launcells Church.** Interesting features of this delightfully situated building include the chancel floor of fifteenth-century Barnstaple encaustic tiles, the early Norman double-cable front and the monument to Sir John Chamond of 1624. But even more interesting are the splendid carved bench-ends with representations of various incidents in the life of Christ.

III. To Widemouth, Crackington Haven and Week St Mary

The coast road to the south runs along the cliffs, providing superb panoramas, to the popular bathing resort of Widemouth Bay (*Brocks-moor*, *Trelawny*). From here the road climbs steeply past Wanson Mouth and in places is difficult but the views are magnificent and all around are broom, gorse and heather. Most motorists do not take their cars down to Millook but park them at the top of the hill, for the descent is steep, 1 in 3, and the lane rather narrow. Millook is at the opening of the Trebarfoote Coombe, a beautifully wooded glen. The beach is stony but the strangely contorted cliffs are interesting.

The road continues to **Crackington Haven** (*Coombe Barton*) at the mouth of an extremely picturesque valley, flanked by towering cliffs and thickly covered with heather, bracken and wild flowers. There is a good surfing beach and a few hotels and guest-houses.

A mile above the Haven is a road at a fork which leads to **St Gennys,** ½ mile inland. The church, finely situated on a slope high above the sea, is dedicated to St Genesius, a martyr who is said to have carried his head after decapitation. The sturdy low tower is Norman, though the upper storey with its pinnacles is a restoration. The square font dates from the twelfth century.

The coastline near Crackington Haven is most impressive. To the north rise Pencannow Point (400 feet) and beyond that Dizzard Point (nearly 500 feet). To the south is Cambeak (330 feet).

The road running eastward from Crackington Haven joins the A39 Bude–Tintagel road in about 3 miles. Turn left towards Bude and then shortly right for **Jacobstow.** The church lying in a wooded hollow contains a massive Norman font with faces at the four corners and flowers in niches on the four sides. The pulpit is formed from ancient bench-ends.

The road runs north-east from Jacobstow through the hamlet of Dinnicoombe to meet the Poundstock–Week St Mary road. Here turn right for **Week St Mary,** a typical upland North Cornish village (540 feet above sea level), looking far more remote than its accessibility warrants. The church has traces of Norman and Early English masonry in the walls. In the north aisle, once a chantry, a piscina and a few fragments of an altar remain and the rood-loft stairway may still be seen. The octagonal granite font is late Gothic.

Take the road northward from Week St Mary which leads in 5 miles to **Marhamchurch.** It is a fascinating village, the church standing beyond a wide square flanked by thatched cottages. The pulpit, richly carved, dates from the time of Charles II. Note the fine square font and rare four-holed cresset stone, also the Delabole slate floor of packed square slates set on end. In the fifteenth century an anchoress named Cecilia Moyes occupied a hut attached to the north wall of the sanctuary (the church was cruciform in those days) and the window in the wall through which she used to watch the service and take her communion is embodied in a small window at the west end of the north aisle.

Bude lies 2 miles north of Marhamchurch.

Bude to Wadebridge

The direct route is by the main A39 road which runs in a south-westerly direction some distance from the coast. A much more interesting though leisurely route is to turn off right, after 12 miles, at Tresparrett Posts and journey by the coast road visiting Boscastle and Tintagel, before rejoining the main road at Camelford.

Leave Bude by the A39 and in 5 miles a right turn leads to **Poundstock,** delightfully placed, with its church of St Neot in a sheltered hollow. Note the Norman holy-water stoup in the porch, the square Norman–Transitional font and the wall paintings which are unfortunately very faded. The Guildhouse just below the church is a beautiful fourteenth-century building now used for parochial purposes.

Return to the main road and in 7 miles bear right along the B3263 to Boscastle.

Boscastle

Bathing A rock pool on south side of harbour mouth. Swimmers generally prefer Bossiney (2 miles).

Car Parks Near bridge and at entrance to roads leading out to harbour. Also inland at foot of Penally Hill.

Distances Bude, 15 miles; Camelford, 6; Launceston, 20; London, 235; Tintagel, 3.

Early Closing Thursday.

Hotel *Bottreaux House.*

Boscastle consists of a number of houses scattered on a steep hillside and along a deep, picturesque valley, down which rushes a stream. This charming old-world village is practically hidden by trees from those passing down to the harbour by the main road, which runs roughly parallel to it. For this reason, most people passing through, or who are only staying for an hour or so, miss it altogether. It is well worth exploring. It is the wonderful little haven and land-locked harbour that fascinates visitors. So land-locked is it that it is necessary to walk some distance seaward from the parking places, to catch a glimpse of the ocean.

It seems as if the mighty cliffs had determined that the sea should not enter, but a narrow passage has been won, first round the base of one cliff, then round the foot of another. After this double bend, a little harbour is reached. The harbour is of very ancient origin. The outer mole was destroyed by a mine in 1941 but has since been rebuilt with granite blocks from the old Laira Bridge at Plymouth.

The **Museum of Witchcraft** (*April to mid-October, daily 10–9; charge*) houses exhibits relating to the practice of the black art past and present.

Many lovers of Cornwall claim that the coast scenery of Boscastle is unequalled in wild and rugged beauty and variety. From the Bridge there is a path on each side of the stream. That on the left leads to the **Bathing Pool** and **Willapark,** with its coastguard look-out, while at the extremity of the right-hand walk the headland which guards the entrance to the haven can be climbed. Good views of the adjacent cliffs are revealed at every turn. Note the profile rock from above the bathing-

Boscastle

pool. The little island out at sea is **Meachard.** There is a blow-hole in the harbour—a natural hole through the narrow neck of land leading out to Penally Head. At certain states of tide, particularly with an off-sea wind, water surges through the hole with a terrific roaring noise and a jet of spray and foam is thrown across the harbour entrance. The harbour and much of the surrounding coast land is National Trust property.

Forrabury Church (St Symphorian), on the top of the hill inland, has a worn, weather-beaten appearance. It can be reached by a footpath across Forrabury Common from Willapark. Its situation is magnificent, and it contains many features of interest, including the south porch, with roof of granite slabs, and the bench-ends in the altar table. South of the churchyard, by the road, is a fine old cross, 5 feet 7 inches high.

The Valency Valley

The deep combe in which Boscastle stands is watered by the rivers Valency and Jordan, affording good trout-fishing. The valley scenery is charming, one side thickly wooded, the other bare. This, the favourite inland walk from Boscastle, extends for about 3 miles, and is entered beyond the bridge, a signboard by 'Checklands', at the foot of Penally Hill, indicating the path. If one part of the valley can be said to be more beautiful than another it is where a second cleft in the hill leads off on the right. At the head of the last-mentioned valley is **Minster Church,** in a romantic situation. A priory once existed here, of which the church formed part. **Lesnewth Valley,** another lovely spot, is a mile or so farther on. The explorer of these valleys will also want to visit St **St Juliot,** with a church containing a fine carved barrel roof and three old crosses in the graveyard. It is of interest to admirers of Thomas Hardy, who, as a young man, was the architect in charge of the church restoration, and married, as his first wife, the rector's sister-in-law to whom, after her death, Hardy erected a memorial in the church.

A long and steep climb out of Boscastle leads to the hamlet of **Tre-valga.** The church shows traces of Norman work in the lower masonry and the font is Norman. Near the porch is an ancient cross 5 feet 8 inches high. On the nearby cliff is a holed rock which is known as the Ladies' Window.

In a further mile we reach **Bossiney** which, though now of no importance, has figured prominently in political life. Until the Reform Act of 1832 Bossiney, in conjunction with Tintagel, returned two members to Westminster. The electors numbered 25, but nine only, belonging to one family, exercised the franchise. Bossiney is now a quiet resort and at Bossiney beach the best bathing in the area may be had. Here stands a natural arch known as the Elephant Rock, because the pillar is supposed to resemble an elephant's trunk. The story goes that under Castle Hill is buried the Round Table: on Midsummer's Eve it rises from the earth and shines like silver. About ½ mile south-east of Bossiney is the Celtic **Pentaly Cross.**

Tintagel

Bathing At Bossiney Cove, Tintagel Cove and Trebarwith Strand.
Buses To Bude, Camelford and Wadebridge.
Distances Bodmin, 20 miles; Boscastle, 3; Camelford, 5; Launceston, 21;
London 232; Wadebridge, 16.
Early Closing Wednesday (not summer)
Hotels *Bossiney House; Atlantic View; Eirenikon; El Condado; Pengenna.*
Population 1,372.

Tintagel is situated some 330 feet above the sea and though the village at first sight is not very impressive it improves on acquaintance. The cliff walks disclose some of the finest coastal scenery and there is bathing at Bossiney. On the left of the road leading through the village is the **Old Post Office** built in the fourteenth century as a manor house but used as a letter receiving office from 1844 to 1892. It is owned by the National Trust. *Open April to October, weekdays 11–1, 2–6, Sunday 2– 6; charge.*

For Tintagel Castle and Cove (about ⅛ mile distant) take the second lane on the left, where the road bears sharply to the right, near the end of the village. The way down is clearly indicated. The lane is impracticable for cars but there are several car parks.

Tintagel Castle
Open: March, April and October, weekdays 9.30–5.30, Sunday 2–5; May to September, weekdays 9.30–7, Sunday 2–7; November to February, weekdays 9.30–4, Sunday 2–4
History The earliest remains are those of the Celtic monastery, dating between the fifth and ninth centuries and already in ruins when the Castle was built. The Great Hall and Chapel were erected by Reginald, Earl of Cornwall, at the time when Tintagel is first mentioned by Geoffrey of Monmouth (1141–75).

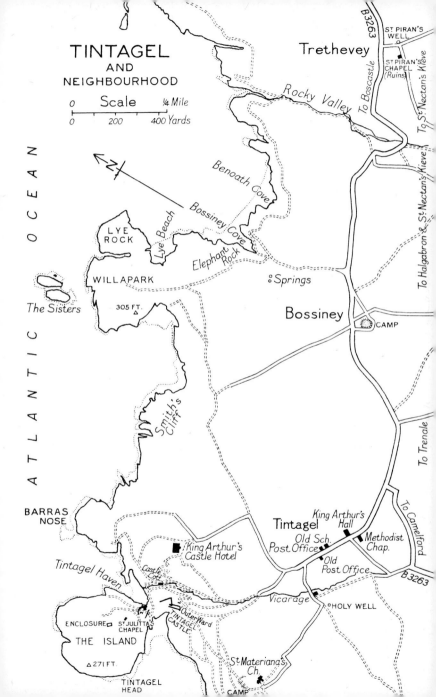

Tintagel was then alienated and only recovered by Richard, the brother of Henry III, in 1235. He increased the strength of the Castle, building the Outer Ward on the mainland and the Curtain enclosing the courtyard and the iron gate covering the seaward approach on the island. In 1245 David, Prince of North Wales, was the guest, at Tintagel, of Richard, Earl of Cornwall, King of the Romans. Several governors were appointed but the dilapidations of time received no attention from them. In fact, about the year 1330, John, Earl of Cornwall, caused the great hall, which was partly in ruins, to be demolished. Subsequently this royal residence became a prison in the charge of a constable, and numbered among its prisoners one John of Northampton, Lord Mayor of London. The early historians of the county, Leland, Carew, and others, all refer to the castle as being in complete ruin in the middle of the sixteenth century. Leland records that between the present Outer Ward and the Castle some long elm trees were placed across the chasm to form a bridge. Since those days the distance between the two cliffs has become more pronounced, owing to the action of the weather.

Though Arthur was a historical figure, nothing has been found during excavations to give archaeological support to any special connection with Tintagel but the mere fact that it has been for so many centuries the traditional centre of the legend adds a mantle of romance to its inherent grandeur.

On arriving at the Cove a few yards after passing the café on the right and the Custodian's office on the left, the **Beach** of dark sand and slaty pebbles is seen below, with the vast mass of **Tintagel Head** towering above to the left. To descend to the beach follow the path to the left for a few yards when the steps will be seen on the right. There is also a less secure way down on the right.

Gazing upwards from the beach the wild and rugged grandeur of the great headland (rising to some 270 feet) is impressive in the extreme— without doubt an ideal site for a medieval fortress. At the base and piercing the great cliff is **Merlin's Cave,** through which access is gained to the miniature beach on the south side of the headland, if the tide is low. It is advisable to make sure that the water is still receding before venturing through.

Tintagel Head is connected to the mainland by a short, narrow isthmus, but is likely to become an island before many years have passed. In 1820, and again in 1846, great masses of cliff fell away, leaving the remains of the Castle precariously clinging to the very edge of the headland. Hereabouts was the site of the ancient **Drawbridge.**

The Castle site was explored and various excavations made by the Ministry of Works in 1933–6. Their conclusions were that the Castle dates from the twelfth century and that, prior to that time, a Celtic religious settlement existed on the headland.

To visit the ruins of the **Norman Stronghold,** so rich in legend and romance, commence the ascent by the winding foot-path (beyond the steps leading down to the beach) and cross the 'Bridge' over the isthmus which leads up steeply, by steps and railing, to the **Entrance Door.** Those who make the effort will be amply rewarded by the magnificent views in all directions, with the added interest and satisfaction of visiting what is left of one of the most romantic strongholds of ancient times.

The date over the entrance (1852) refers to the year when the Castle was first opened to the public. This doorway gives access to **The Precincts.** The large structure on the right is known as the **Norman Hall,** inside which is a smaller building some 12 feet high. The latter is said to date from the fourteenth century and is believed to have been used for the safe keeping of State prisoners. The scattered ruins of the twelfth-century fortifications, fragments of buildings and some stone steps of a winding stairway are seen on the right. It is possible to trace the area of **The Courtyard** and to follow the curtain of **Battlements,** at least for some of their length. Like the **Iron Gate** (a one-time fortified landing-place) this Curtain is believed to date from the thirteenth century. On the Plateau forming the centre of the 'island' are the remains of the **Chapel of St Julitta,** probably a Norman building, around which can be traced the outline of still earlier enclosures. Beyond, may be seen the **Castle Well** and a rectangular enclosure, the remains of what is believed to have been a medieval garden.

What is left of the **Lower Ward** on the mainland (referred to in an earlier paragraph), can be reached by the steps opposite the Island or the steep path which begins by the side of the Custodian's Office.

The Church of St Materiana is perched on the top of the cliffs overlooking Tintagel 'island' and can be seen for miles around. This is a terribly exposed position; even the tombstones have to be buttressed against the fury of Atlantic gales. Within, the church, with its impressive gloom, is strangely peaceful in contrast. It is unusually interesting, even for a Cornish church, and this in spite of a careful but over-thorough 'restoration' in 1870. The carved font and the south doorway are Norman, while the north doorway has several Saxon features. There is a well-preserved medieval stone altar in the Lady chapel. A milestone, found some years ago, bearing an inscription which may refer to the Emperor Licinius, the brother-in-law of Constantine the Great, is in the south transept. Note the mutilated fifteenth-century rood screen; also the thirteenth-century memorial slab on the floor near the lectern. The brass effigy is fifteenth-century. The outside ironwork of the north door is noteworthy; the hinges are Early English, thought to date from about 1225.

King Arthur's Hall, in the village, was built as headquarters of the Fellowship of the Round Table and is constructed entirely of Cornish stone. At one end of the Hall granite steps lead up to a granite throne, above which is a large block of granite supported by pillars of different varieties of the same rock. Upon this rests a stone with an anvil into which is set a sword, representing the test which the youthful Arthur successfully passed and so proved his right of kingship over all the ambitious aspirants to the throne. Before the throne is a Round Table of granite, and at the other end of the Hall is one of oak. There is an interesting collection of ancient manuscripts and a library of Arthurian literature which is probably the most complete in the world.

Excursions from Tintagel

Trebarwith Strand. This charming spot, popular for picnicking and bathing, may be reached *via* Treknow or by footpath. It is 1½ miles south of Tintagel. The approach by road is romantic, running down between steep hillsides littered with quarry debris and thickly clothed with bracken, heather, and numerous wild flowers. The strand is nearly a mile long at low tide, and there is hotel accommodation. The vast walls of cliff, the caves, sands, and sea, with the Gull Rock conspicuous in the distance, make a fine scene. The bathing and surfing are excellent, except at high tide.

St Nectan's Kieve and the **Rocky Valley.** A visit here should on no account be omitted, for such beautiful sylvan scenery is wholly unsuspected so close to wild Tintagel. Follow the road past King Arthur's Hall (avoiding turn to right), soon passing through Bossiney. The road then descends steeply (1 in 9) to a bridge crossing a stream.

(*a*) On the left at the approach to the bridge is a farm-gate which is the entrance to the public path going down the **Rocky Valley,** the haunt of the raven and the (now very rare) Cornish Chough. The scenery is extremely beautiful, with huge rocks, trees, ferns, wild flowers, and a noisy brook. Half-way down is a ruined mill where on the rock face there are carved two mazes or cabalistic signs which may have some early magical significance. There is no certainty about their meaning.

(b) Perhaps the pleasantest route to the Kieve and Waterfall is through the fields, turning off to the right over a stile by a farmyard at the beginning of Bossiney. The path leads through another farm, crosses the road and descends to the thickly-wooded valley. There are direction-boards pointing to the Kieve. Admission to the Waterfall is obtained from the *Hermitage* (*Tea Garden*). The height of the cascade is forty feet, the greater part of which is a sheer drop; the water then rushes through a natural arch to a shorter fall. The return can be made by road or lane over the hill, from which wide spreading views may be obtained.

From Tintagel the B3263 and B3266 lead in 5 miles to—

Camelford

Buses To Wadebridge, St Columb and Newquay; Trewarmett and Trebarwith; Tintagel; Launceston and Port Isaac.

Early Closing Wednesday.
Population 1,554.

Camelford, the 'Camelot' of Tennyson, lies four miles inland from the coast, on the banks of the river Camel.

It is a small and ancient town, quaint and quiet—except for the traffic—and was made a free borough in 1259. The insignia of the extinct corporation are very interesting. The mace was a gift in 1660.

In recent years Camelford has developed as a holiday centre. Its attractions include a fine bracing air coming from the sea on one side and from moorland on the other; convenient access to Boscastle, Tintagel, Brown Willy, and Rough Tor; numerous prehistoric remains on the moor; interesting churches; fine sands at Trebarwith (4¼ miles); and trout-fishing in the Camel and other streams. Quaint corners attract photographers and artists. During the summer, coaches run to nearby places of interest and buses bring the coast and beautiful valley of the Allen, on the verge of the moors, within easy reach. As a moorland resort, Camelford has great possibilities.

At **Slaughter Bridge,** a good mile above the town, legend says the armies of King Arthur and his nephew, Mordred the Usurper, met in 542. Mordred was killed, and the King mortally wounded. The Bridge should be seen from the low ground by the stream, when its antiquity will be apparent. It somewhat resembles the clapper bridges on Dartmoor.

Slaughter Bridge, near Camelford

About 2 miles west of Camelford, off the B3314, is the **Delabole Slate Quarry and Museum** (*May to September, daily 10–6 ; charge*). This quarry was opened in 1555 and is the largest man-made hole in England, being over 500 feet deep and more than 1½ miles in circumference.

Excursions from Camelford

I. To Lanteglos, Advent and St Teath
A pleasant excursion can be made to the little village of **Lanteglos-by-Camelford** (*Lanteglos Farmhouse*), about a mile to the south. Few people who stay any time in the locality fail to visit Lanteglos church, which is the mother church of Camelford. It is beautifully situated amid trees. The church has traces of Norman masonry. The fine tower was erected in the fifteenth century, and the font is of the same period. Note the round-headed sedilia in the chancel and fifteenth-century glass showing Christ and His Apostles in the upper lights of the aisle win-

dows; also the top of a round-headed cross and remains of stone tracery preserved at the west end of the church, and the tombstone dated 1560. In the churchyard are four old crosses and an ancient Saxon pillar stone found at Castle Goff in 1876.

At **Castle Goff,** a little west of Lanteglos church, are ancient fortifications. The road which encircles the church, turning up at the southeast corner of the graveyard, leads to the hamlet of **Helstone,** which proudly claims to be the place referred to in the Domesday records as having forty brewers!

A passage through an archway in the main street beneath printer's premises leads to a path beside and over the stream. About 2 miles southward by this path is **Advent Parish Church** (St Athewenna), containing a circular Norman font and some ancient memorials. The tall unbuttressed tower, granite arcade and north windows are fourteenth-century, and porch and wagon roofs, beautifully carved, are late fifteenth century. A mile farther south is the **Devil's Jump,** two huge piles of granite one on either side of a deep ravine. It is a weird spot, and many are the legends told of it. The whole district of Camelford, indeed, is rich in antiquities and ancient lore. On the Tresinney estate is an ancient cross with shaft 6 feet 9 inches high.

St Teath, south of Camelford, 2 miles beyond Helstone, has an ancient church rebuilt on a Norman fabric in the fifteenth century. The pulpit is dated 1630. Over a doorway in the tower is a similar date, but this only refers to the doorway itself. There are numerous memorials within the building, some fine bench-ends and a fifteenth-century greenstone font. In the churchyard annexe is a fine old cross, 13 feet high, the second highest in the county. Captain William Bligh, famed master of the *Bounty*, was born in St Teath in 1753.

II. To Rough Tor and Brown Willy

To reach Rough Tor and Brown Willy from Camelford town, go over the bridge and in a few minutes bear off on the right along the ascending road leading to within ¾ mile of the heights. The path is clear but in wet weather becomes difficult. Rough Tor is first reached. Brown Willy is 1¼ miles beyond. The bog between them should be carefully noted and avoided. The distance from Camelford is about 5 miles. The return can be pleasantly varied by walking on from Brown Willy to the Bodmin–Launceston road, there getting a bus to Bodmin and so back to Camelford. The main road is struck not far from Bolventor. **Brown Willy,** 1,375 feet (the highest point in Cornwall), and its near neighbour,

Rocks on Rough Tor, on Bodmin Moor

Rough Tor (pronounced like bough), 1,312 feet, are the two principal heights of Bodmin Moor. The scenery is wildly grand, rugged and bleak. At the top of Rough Tor (N.T.) are some magnificently piled rocks.

III. To Launceston

Leave Camelford by the A39 Bude road and in 3 miles branch right along the A395 which leads in a further 14 miles to—

Launceston

Angling There is good angling on the Tamar, the Inney and other streams in the area.

Baths Swimming pool in Coronation Park.

Bowls Two clubs welcome visitors: Kensey Vale and Dunheved.

Buses To Tavistock and Plymouth; Wadebridge and Newquay; Bideford and Bude.

Distances Bodmin, 22 miles; Bude, 19; Camelford, 17; London, 211; Plymouth, 27.

Early Closing Thursday.

Golf *Launceston Golf Club*, St Stephens.

Hotel *Eagle House.*

Population 5,300.

Tennis Courts in Coronation Park.

Often described as 'The Gateway to Cornwall owing to its position just across the border from Devon, the town stands high above its immediate surroundings, in the centre of some of the finest moorland scenery in the west of England.

Launceston (one time capital of the county), is an ancient place, with the indefinable atmosphere of a cathedral city. It is the *Lauscavetone* of Domesday, and is also known by its Norman title of *Dunheved* meaning 'a city on a hill.' Dunheved was incorporated as a free borough by Richard, Earl of Cornwall, and the borough had a mayor as early as 1257. In 1259 it returned two members to Parliament.

The chief attraction to visitors is **Launceston Castle** (*March, April and October, weekdays 9.30–5.30, Sunday 2–5 ; May to September, weekdays 9.30–7, Sunday 2–7 ; November to February, weekdays 9.30–4, Sunday 2–4*). This is a grand old ruin commanding splendid views and surrounded by pleasant grounds and is only a few minutes' walk from the centre of the town. From the War Memorial go to the west end of the Square, and turn down to the right for 150 yards. The Keep is almost all that remains, and the approach from the grounds is up a long flight of stone steps. The view from the doorways and pathways surrounding the Keep is astonishing. The climb up to the town seems onerous enough, yet from the Castle we look down at it from quite a dizzy height. The wide view

Launceston Castle

is particularly impressive to the west, where the heights of Bodmin Moor, Brown Willy and Rough Tor break against the skyline. The north gate, which is not within the fenced-off portion, is the best preserved part, with a room on one side. A notice states that George Fox, founder of the Society of Friends, was, with other Quakers, immured here ('in Doomsdale') for eight months in 1656, for distributing religious papers in West Cornwall.

The Castle was begun about the time of Edward the Confessor. The original castle was probably of timber. Much of the masonry structure belongs to the first half of the thirteenth century and may be due to Richard, Earl of Cornwall.

Lawrence House, a fine Georgian house in Castle Street owned by the National Trust, houses an interesting local museum (*April to September, Monday to Saturday 2.30–4.30; October, November, February and March, Wednesday 2.30–4.30; free*).

Fragments of **Launceston Priory,** completed in 1140, are still to be seen, notably in the Norman doorway of the *White Hart.*

St Mary Magdalene Church, consecrated in 1524, is a remarkable building. There is scarcely a square foot of its exterior walls that is not decorated with quatrefoils, shields, fleurs-de-lis, Latin inscriptions, coats-of-arms, saints, foliage, and other devices rather coarsely executed.

From the chancel door eastward round the building is a Latin inscription, beginning 'Ave Maria'. The fine porch has an upper chamber. In front are the weather-worn arms of Trecarell and Kelway and the date 1511. The tower is fourteenth-century. The church has some notable woodwork, new and old; note the screen, the roof, the pulpit, and the bench-ends. The font is old, though re-tooled. There are many interesting memorials.

On the north side of the churchyard note on a tombstone the ancient cross head. The shaft is modern.

St Thomas's Church, though not as ornate as St Mary's, has many features of interest, including a very beautiful square font, probably brought from the Priory, fine pillars and arches, and good linen-fold panelling. The church appears to have been connected officially with the Castle, for felons were buried in the churchyard, and there were many references to judicial proceedings in the church accounts.

The Early English **South Gate** of the town, a fine structure, remains. The rooms in the upper storey were once used as the town 'lock-up'.

The **Windmill,** a fine open space, approached from the Square by way of Westgate Street and a steep hill, stands 585 feet above sea-level and commands magnificent views in all directions. Below the Windmill is the Coronation Park with swimming baths and tennis courts.

Leave Launceston by the A30 Bodmin road, keeping left in 3 miles. In a further 5 miles a right turn leads to **Altarnun.** The name Altarnun means 'The Altar of St Nonna', a Cornish saint, patron also of a parish in Brittany. There is a beautiful cross in the churchyard, and the Norman font, fifteenth-century high tower, fifteenth-century carved wagon roofs and rood screen are striking features. The greatest treasures of the church, however, are the magnificent solid bench-ends. They are 79 in number and are most richly carved with the Instruments of the Passion, a man with a cauldron, a man playing bagpipes, a fiddler, etc.

Follow the moorland road north-west from Altarnun through the hamlet of West Carne to a T-junction at Newpark. The right turn leads in about 3 miles to **St Clether,** which is notable for a beautiful example of the little wayside chapels which were numerous in pre-Norman times. Nearly all of them were destroyed at the Reformation, but this one, built in the fifteenth century on the site of an earlier one, was spared, although it became ruined. It was beautifully restored, and fortunately its most interesting feature remains as it was in the past; that is, the little stream which flows from the beautiful Holy Well into the chapel, passing behind the stone altar, and out through a recess in the opposite wall into a second well.

The left turn at Newpark joins the A39 2 miles north-east of Camelford.

IV. To Michaelstow and St Breward

Along the valley of the Camel, which is roughly followed by the Camelford—Bodmin road, are many interesting villages with picturesque churches and cottages. The valley forms the western side of the moors, so that, with the exception of St Breward and Blisland (which is described in connection with Bodmin) most of the villages are on the western side of the valley.

Michaelstow is reached by turning to the right from the Camelford—Bodmin road (B3266) about 2½ miles from the Wadebridge fork. The church lies at the back of a pleasant chained green, and, with a magnificent cross, a well in the churchyard, a stone porch with narrow arch, Tudor doorway, octagonal font and handsome bench-ends, is beautiful in itself and is set in lovely surroundings.

St Breward is reached by a poor but picturesque road which turns left from B3266, half a mile beyond Michaelstow. The church has traces of five circular Norman pillars on the north side, made of large slabs of granite, while the south pillars are fluted, with a flat arch.

It makes a pleasant round to continue from St Breward through **Row** and **Lank** (near the De Lank quarries), to cross the Camel again at Wenford bridge, with china clay works a mile to the south, and to climb up to **St Tudy.** This is a pretty, open village with a little green in front of the church, which has some old monuments, a Transition font and very fine carved work in the porch. One of its most interesting features is the coped stone, one of only 30 in England, of Hiberno-Saxon origin, which was found deeply buried in the churchyard and now, with explanatory notes, is carefully preserved in the porch.

From St Tudy the Bodmin road may be regained and return made direct to Camelford. It is more interesting, however, to continue southward for rather less than two miles and turn to the right at Longstone cross-roads, reaching **St Mabyn** in another mile.

From St Mabyn continue down a steep hill to cross the river Allen, emerging on to the Camelford–Wadebridge road near St Kew Highway.

Leave Camelford by the A39 Wadebridge Road. In 12 miles at St Kew Highway turn right for the picturesque village of **St Kew** in its beautiful wooded vale. The church is particularly interesting.

Beautifully plain, without plaster, its attractions include the windows of rare old painted glass. One, in the north chapel, dating from about 1469, depicts our Lord's Passion; over this window are the arms of Henry V, for in medieval times there was a King's Chapel and priest at St Kew. In the south chapel are the fragments of a Jesse window. There is also some old glass in one or two windows in the aisle. All of the old roof timbers and four bench-ends remain; the modern screen incorporates a portion of the original, and the pulpit is Elizabethan. Note the coloured plaster Royal Arms (1661) with a fearsome lion and 'God Save the King,' and the ringers' rhyme-board in the base of the tower. There are also stocks, a Cornish cross, by the church steps, a rare fifteenth-century lantern cross, and an interesting old almsbox, while the 'Ogham' stone inscribed IUSTI is probably fifth century. The Ogham writing of the Gaels consists of combinations of straight lines, which are seen on the edge of the stone.

Return to the main road and in a further 2 miles at Three Holes Cross a track runs eastward to **Castle Killibury,** a prehistoric hill fort and possibly the original Killiwick of Arthurian romance.

In a further mile we reach—

Wadebridge

Boating On the River Camel.
Bowls, Tennis and Putting At Egloshayle.
Distances Boscastle, 17 miles; Camelford, 11; London, 238; Newquay, 16; Truro, 24.
Early Closing Wednesday.
Hotel *Molesworth Arms.*
Population 3,553.

Wadebridge stands at the head of the Camel estuary, about 8 miles from the sea—a clean and bright town, rapidly increasing in popularity. The river scenery, particularly above the town, is beautiful, the waters winding between wooded hills, the latter contrasting with the exposed hills seawards. The name of the town is said to be derived from the Roman *Vadum*, a ford.

The **Bridge,** originally 510 feet long, of 17 pointed Gothic arches, had angles over each pier as refuges for pedestrians against the traffic. Four of the original arches are now blocked up, three under the road at the town side and one beneath the eastern approach. In 1852–3 the bridge was widened 3 feet on each side by building granite segmental arches thrust out between the cutwaters. As this is, perhaps, the finest example in the British Isles of a 500-year-old bridge still in constant daily use, great care was taken to preserve its appearance during a bridge widening scheme carried out in 1962–3.

Coronation Park on the St Breock side is a lovely natural woodland on the slopes of the Polmorla Valley. At the top of the hill is a war memorial. On the Egloshayle side of the river is a large playing field. Good boating is available and the river scenery is very picturesque. **Polbrock** and **Grogley,** with their woods, are favourite spots for rambles.

Excursions from Wadebridge

I. To Polzeath and Port Isaac

Cross the river by the A39 and in ¼ mile turn left along the B3314. In 3 miles a left turn leads to the popular sailing centre of **Rock,** which is connected by pedestrian ferry with Padstow on the opposite side of the Camel estuary. The St Enodoc golf course is one of the country's finest natural courses.

A mile north of Rock, over the golf links, is the ancient **Church of St Enodoc** (chapel of ease to St Minver), which was threatened with the same fate as St Piran-in-the-Sands. The sands did overwhelm the church, and the building at one time could only be entered through the roof, but happily it has been reclaimed and preserved. There are traces of Norman work and the font is of the same period. Note the holy water stoup at the south entrance, made into an alms-box, and the base of the fifteenth-century screen. The spire is slightly out of the perpendicular.

The mother village of Rock, **St Minver,** lies 2 miles west and the church is well worth a visit. The Perpendicular octagonal font, fine bench-ends, rood stairs and brass to Roger Opy (1517) are particularly interesting. There are traces of Norman masonry in the chancel, and the north aisle has heavy octagonal pillars of flat stones, contrasting with the graceful granite monoliths on the south side. Against the west wall is a Norman capital found in 1927.

North of Rock **Trebetherick, Polzeath** and **Pentireglaze** are popular holiday resorts offering good surfing, cliff scenery and ample accommodation. On **Rumps Point,** the northernmost promontory, are the remains of an Iron Age fortress. Eastward is Portquin Bay with magnificent scenery almost rivalling that at Tintagel. The village of **Portquin** lies in a tiny cove at the extreme eastern end of the bay.

At a cross-roads on the Portquin–St Endellion road is **Long Cross,** the shaft of an ancient cross with the inscription 'Brocagni hic jacet', probably referring to Brechan, a Welsh prince and the father of St Endelienta, the patron saint of the fifteenth-century church in **St Endellion.** Note the holy water stoup, the ornamented south doorway, the Norman font, the bench-ends and the carved wagon roofs. But the most impressive feature is the magnificently sculpted tomb chest in the south aisle dating from about 1400. About ½ mile to the east stands the sixteenth-century farmhouse **Tresungers** with embattled entrance tower.

Port Isaac (*Castle Rock*, *St Andrews*) is a delightfully quaint fishing village and resort 2 miles east of Portquin and 2 miles north of St Endellion. For bathing it is advisable to go to nearby Port Gaverne. There are pleasant modern houses on the hill-top but the oldest part of the port is packed so tightly between the steep hillsides that vehicles get into and out of the village only with some difficulty. Motorists paying a fleeting visit are recommended to leave their cars up above and make their way down on foot.

The return to Wadebridge may be made via St Kew (see page 36).

II. To Egloshayle

Cross the river and at once turn right along the A389 which leads in ½ mile to **Egloshayle Church** pleasantly placed overlooking river meadows. The unplastered walls give the interior an unusually rugged appearance. There is a good wagon roof in the south aisle and the font is Norman. In the base of the fine tower—said to have been built of stone left over from Wadebridge bridge—are remains of a monument to the Kestell family bearing dates from 1520 to 1581.

III. To St Breock

St Breock lies less than a mile south-west of Wadebridge and the church is beautifully situated with a stream running through the churchyard. The lower parts of the tower and the two doorways and two windows at the west end of the nave are fourteenth century, while the font and the two windows in the south aisle date from the fifteenth century. Of the various memorials the oldest, a priest's tomb, at the east end, is early thirteenth century.

At **Nanscow,** 1 mile south of St Breock, is to be seen the tombstone, probably about 1,700 years old, of Ulcagnus, son of Severus. About 1 mile further south near **Pawton** is the megalithic chamber known as Pawton Quoit and other stones of archaeological interest may be seen in the area.

IV. To Bodmin

Leave Wadebridge by the A389 which leads in 7 miles to—

Bodmin

Bowls green near the Barracks.
Cinema *Palace,* Fore Street.
Distances Exeter, 64 miles; Liskeard, 13; London, 234; Newquay, 20; Truro, 25.

Early Closing Wednesday.
Hotel *Westberry.*
Library Lower Bore Street.
Population 10,430.

Bodmin, the county town, is an excellent centre from which to tour Cornwall, being only about 12 miles from north and south coasts and on the south-western fringe of Bodmin Moor, the highest points of which are Brown Willy (1,375 feet) and Rough Tor (1,311 feet).

The town is the headquarters of anglers using the River Camel, a very good trout and salmon stream. It was the county's principal town before the Norman Conquest and has had an interesting and often exciting history—much of it bound up with its Priory before 1539. As a religious centre it owed much to Guron, later canonized, who founded a hermitage in the valley about the year 530. Petroc, his successor, founded a monastery. He was one of the greatest figures, as Abbot and Confessor, in the Celtic Church, and died in 564. He, too, was canonized.

The burgesses are mentioned in a Pipe Roll dated 1190, but until the Dissolution the Prior was lord of the town; the early charters were granted to the Prior and not until the charter granted by Queen Elizabeth I in 1562 was Bodmin a free borough. The last important charter was granted by George III in 1798.

St Petroc's Church, of noble proportions, is the largest parish church in the county. It stands near where the main roads from Launceston and Liskeard enter the town. Norman work in the base of the tower shows that there was an earlier church on the site; but the church standing today was built between 1469 and 1471 by the townspeople, notably helped by their guilds. The fan vaulting in the porch roof is a very good specimen of medieval stone groining. The lectern, made up of parts of the old choir stalls, and the pulpit are fine examples of fifteenth-century carving. The font is an outstanding example of late Norman undercut work and a rare fifteenth-century piscina has been put to use as a collection box. The splendid altar tomb of Prior Vyvyan, the last prior but one before the Dissolution, is on the north side of the sanctuary. It originally stood in front of the high altar of the former Priory Church, of which only a few fragments remain.

In the neighbourhood are remains of several ancient earthworks, including Castle Canyke, Dunmere camp and a Roman camp at Tregear. Near Nanstallon, coins of Vespasian (A.D. 69) and Trajan (A.D. 98–117) were found as well as rings, spearheads and fragments of Roman pottery.

While rich in historical associations, Bodmin is also the centre of much fine and varied scenery, from the wild rolling hills of the moor to the beauties of the Glynn and Camel valleys. **Dunmere Woods** to the north are particularly beautiful with the River Camel running through them.

Excursions from Bodmin
I To Blisland and Dozmary Pool
Leave Bodmin by the A30 Launceston road which, passing over the Racecourse Downs, has magnificent open views. In 3½ miles, at Four Winds, turn left for **Blisland.** The village, one of the most picturesque

Lanhydrock Church, near Bodmin (see page 134)

in Cornwall, has a green shaded by many fine ash and sycamore trees. The Norman church has good wagon roofs and a tower at the north end.

The main road continues through **Temple** where the church stands on the site of a chapel of the Knights-Templars, to **Bolventor** where stands the famous *Jamaica Inn*. Here a right turn leads in 2 miles to **Dozmary Pool.** There is little in the scenery of the pool to justify the excursion, but because of its association with the Arthurian legends it is visited by considerable numbers of people, for here took place the traditional passing of Arthur and the return to the mystic giver of his invincible sword *Excalibur*. There was a story that Dozmary was bottomless, but the pool dried up in 1869 and so disposed of that legend. Some say that Tennyson envisaged the event as happening at Looe Pool near Helston, which better coincides with the scene described in *Morte d'Arthur*.

II To Cardinham

As in the previous excursion take the Launceston road as far as Four Winds cross-roads, and then turn right for **Cardinham.** On a hill stands the fifteenth-century church with three-stage granite tower. Note the fine wagon roofs, the Transition–Norman font, the carved bench-ends and Charles I's letter of thanks. In the churchyard opposite the south door is one of the best Celtic crosses in Cornwall, standing 8½ feet high.

The return journey may be made by the road running south from the church through Fletchersbridge and Turfdown.

Wadebridge to Newquay

From Wadebridge to Newquay is about 16 miles by the main A39 road through St Jidgey and St Columb Major. However the coastal route via Padstow is much more rewarding and will be described here.

Leave Wadebridge by the A39 Newquay road and in 2 miles turn right along the A389 which leads in a further 2 miles to **Little Petherick** charmingly placed at the head of Petherick Creek. The tiny fourteenth-century church was rebuilt in 1858 and is a veritable museum of ecclesiastical treasures, including a Venetian processional cross, a Byzantine altar cross and one of the finest collections of vestments in Cornwall.

Padstow

Bathing There are bathing beaches at Chapel Bar, Ship-my-Pumps, below Chapel Stile (town beach), St George's Cove and Harbour Cove (Tregirls Beach).
Bowls Nine rinks at the Dinas Hotel.
Distances Bodmin, 15 miles; London, 246; Newquay, 15; Tintagel, 21; Wadebridge, 8.
Ferry Pedestrian ferry across the Camel estuary to Rock (for the golf course) sails from North Quay.
Fishing Fairly good fishing for bass etc. from boats. Fine area for mackerel.
Golf *Trevose Golf Club* at Constantine and *St Enedoc Golf Club* at Rock.
Hotels *Dinas, Gulland Rock, Metropole.*
Population 2,802.
Tennis Public courts at the Lawn Car Park.

Scattered down the slopes and at the foot of a steep cliff is the ancient port of Padstow (formerly Petrockstow). It was once a corporate borough governed by a mayor and burgesses with a charter granted in 1583 by Queen Elizabeth. It developed into a ship-building port of some importance, but steam and, later, motor vessels gradually replaced the old Padstow schooners. The trade of the port was at one time largely with Canada for timber; later fishing, chiefly for soles, became the principal business. Now it is a residential country town and shopping centre for a wide area.

Padstow is also a thriving holiday resort. There is first-class sailing and boating, the chief drawbacks being swift tides and erratic breezes, greater hindrances to the novice than to the experienced. Owing to the position of Padstow on a peninsula, a great many different coves and bays can be easily visited. In the season daily coach excursions are run to all parts and there are daily cruises round the several headlands and small islands off the coast. The Tropical Bird Gardens (*daily 10.30–dusk ; charge*) house about 200 different species of birds.

St Petroc's Church is of great interest although it has been extensively restored. The stained-glass windows are fine and the fifteenth-century font has sculptured figures of the twelve apostles. The thirteenth-century tower is much older than the rest of the building which was enlarged and rebuilt in the fifteenth century. In the south aisle is a fifteenth-century carved sedilia made of four of the old bench-ends, two of which are in excellent preservation. The pulpit is sixteenth-century or possibly pre-Reformation and finely preserved. The rood-stairs will be noticed and some old bosses of the roof; also the angels on the wall plates in the south chapel. There are numerous memorials, a striking one (at west end of south aisle) being to members of the Prideaux family. The ancient stocks are in the south porch.

Padstow possesses many quaint corners, narrow and crooked by-ways and picturesque buildings. In Fentonluna Lane (*Monastery Well*), leading to Prideaux Place, is a renovated **Well,** now marked by a pump bearing the date 1592 on a modern stone at the top, with older lettering round the sides, on which 'Prideau' and 'Nicholas' may be read. Parallel to Fentonluna is the so-called High Street, an amazing little narrow lane tumbling down towards the Quay. On the North quay is an ancient building known as **Abbey House,** from which a subterranean passage was built to connect it with the monastery (destroyed by the Danes in 981) which formerly occupied the upper part of the town, including Prideaux Place. It is believed to have been the old Guild House of the Padstow merchants and dates from the fifteenth century. It contains some odd bits of stone tracery. **Raleigh's Court House,** on the South quayside, dates back to the sixteenth century. Here Raleigh held his Court and collected his legal dues as Warden of Cornwall. At the top of the hill is the imposing Prideaux Place (*private*). Its castellated façade is of great length and very beautiful.

Padstow Hobby-Horse. A quaint custom and a rite of great antiquity is the 'hobby horse' dance held on May Day. The hobby-horse is a fearsome creature, with its ferocious mask, and more like a heathen god than a horse. Before the horse dances a man carrying a club called the 'Teaser'. The whole thing is grotesque, but is one of the most genuine folk customs surviving in England. In Cross Street will be noticed a cross let into the pavement. In the centre of this a maypole used to be set up as part of the 'hobby-horse' celebrations. Now the maypole is set up in the Market Square.

Excursions from Padstow

I. The Camel Estuary

Were it not for the sand bar at the mouth this natural harbour would be of greater use to mariners. The estuary, winding between grassy cliffs on one side and the lower sandy dunes on the other, is always beautiful, but especially so at high water. It averages about ¾ of a mile in width, and is over 6 miles long. The entrance is guarded by **Pentire Point** (Rock side) and **Stepper Point** (Padstow side). The latter, 227 feet high, is surmounted by a small tower, or 'day-mark', for shipping. It is a pretty walk of 2½ miles from Padstow by the path down the estuary to the Day-mark; starting from the harbour or turning to the right at the fork of the main street up the town, the two paths converging at the War Memorial Cross overlooking the estuary. A short distance before this a path turns down to the cove on the shore, which is the low-tide starting-place of the **Rock Ferry.** Continuing, the way soon drops down to the rocky inlet of **St George's Well,** a perennially flowing spring in the rocks. Crossing the little stream, the path climbs steeply to **Gun Point,** then continues to **Harbour Cove,** locally known as Tregirls Beach, with fine sands, affording a fine view of the **Doom Bar.**

Month by month thousands of tons of sand are taken from the estuary for agricultural purposes, as it is rich in carbonate of lime. This has provided a considerable export activity for many years.

From the head of Harbour Cove the path can be followed along the coast past **Hawker's Cove** to Stepper Point, whence the walk may be continued round the coast to **Gunver Head,** or a return made to Padstow by striking up the path which follows the cliffs by Lelizzick Farm. Now on to Crugmeer and then by the old church path direct to Padstow or by road to Trethillick and Padstow.

A word must be said respecting the fine cliff scenery of the neighbourhood. The **Tregudda Gorge** is a grand sight at any time, and magnificent when the sea is rough. The gorge lies between three very fine sea stacks and the mainland.

II. Trevose Head and St Merryn

Trevose Head and lighthouse are well worth the 5-mile journey from Padstow. Leave by the B3276 and in 2 miles a right turn leads to Harlyn Bay which has a good sandy beach between headlands. There is also a prehistoric burial site here with an interesting museum. The cliff path goes from Harlyn Bay to the Head or the toll road may be taken. **Trevose Head** is only 243 feet high, but the view along the coast is wonderful, past Bedruthan, Porth, Newquay, and even as far as St Ives on a very clear day. The headland is a fine mass of jagged rock and the cliff scenery all round is grand and imposing. The islets lying some way off are the Quies Rocks.

The return may be made via **St Merryn** where the church contains the font from the ruined church of St Constantine a mile to the west. It is a fine specimen of fourteenth-century work, similar to that at Padstow. The old stocks are in the porch.

Continuing the journey to Newquay leave Padstow by the B3276 passing through St Merryn and reaching the sea at Porthcothan. In a further 2½ miles a car park is reached from which a short walk enables one to view from the cliffs **Bedruthan Steps.** Legend says that these huge detached masses were stepping stones for the giant Bedruthan. Queen Bess, one of the most prominent, is said to bear a resemblance to the Virgin Queen when viewed from the right angle. There are numerous large waterworn caverns. Bedruthan looks its best towards sunset when the rocks assume glorious colours.

Continue along the main road to Watergate Bay (*Cleavelands*, *Tregurrian*) where a deep cleft between hills leads to a magnificent stretch of sand with superb cliff scenery. Newquay may easily be reached by a walk along the sands

Newquay

Bathing Excellent at all states of the tide. Extensive sands, clean and firm, but bathers should be cautioned against approaching rocks, especially in Fistral Bay. Bathing at low water on any beach is very unwise.

Beaches All of fine tide-washed sand. The largest is Fistral Beach, south-west of the Headland. North-east of it and directly below the main parts of the town

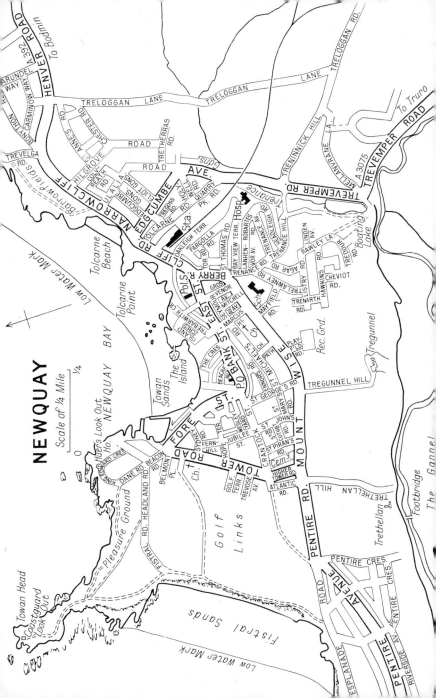

are Towan, Great Western (Bothwicks), Tolcarne and other beaches.

Boating Motor and other boats are on hire in the Harbour. There is also boating on the River Gannel and Trenance Valley boating lake.

Bowls In Trenance Gardens and Eothen Green.

Buses Services to almost every part of Cornwall mainly from the bus station in East Street.

Cinemas *Astor*, Narrowcliff; *Victoria*, Chapel Hill; *Camelot*, The Crescent.

Distances Bodmin, 20 miles; London, 254; Padstow, 15; Redruth, 16; St Austell, 16; Truro, 16; Wadebridge, 16.

Early Closing Wednesday.

Fishing Good sea fishing from boats and from the rocks. Full facilities for deep-water shark fishing. Information from the harbour master.

Golf *Newquay Golf Club* above Fistral Bay.

Hotels *Atlantic; Barrowfield; Bay; Beachcroft, Bewdley; Bristol; Corisande Manor; Glendorgal; Great Western; Headland; Hotel Riviera; Kilbirnie; La Hotel Felica; Marina; Red Lion; St Rumon's Bay; Sandy Lodge; Trebarwith; Trevelgue; Waters Edge; Windsor.*

Information Centre Morfa Hall, Cliff Road.

Library Marcus Hill.

Population 13,890.

Swimming Pools Indoor and outdoor heated pools at Trenance Park.

Tennis Public courts at Trenance Gardens and Mount Wise.

Theatres *Cosy Nook Theatre*, Towan Promenade; *Newquay Theatre*, St Michael's Road.

Newquay is the largest and most popular holiday resort on the north coast of Cornwall. It lies midway between Bude and Land's End, 281 miles by rail from London, 254 by road, and 14 miles north of Truro. At this point of the coast Towan Head projects north-westward and with Pentire Headland and Trevelgue Head forms two spacious sandy bays. The principal portion of Newquay has been built along the cliffs overlooking the more easterly of these two bays, and the eastward expansion still goes on; but the town has rapidly taken command of the wide western bay, and has also spread itself over the northern slopes of the ridge of high ground known as Mount Wise. Many of the houses here have excellent views in all directions: northward over Newquay to the Headland and the sea, southward over the luxuriant valley of the Gannel.

In former times Newquay was merely a little fishing village, practically unknown except for its catches of pilchards. A century ago its population could hardly have totalled a hundred; in 1871 it had risen to 1,121. The population now numbers over 13,000.

The railway which put Newquay in touch with the rest of the world dates only from 1875. Once given the opportunity, the public quickly showed their appreciation of Newquay cliff scenery, the charm of its vast sands, and the purity and brilliant colouring of its sea, gracious and lovely in fine weather, and magnificent when the wind blows hard from the west and north, or when the Atlantic sweeps in line upon line and hurls itself against the stern, wild cliffs.

Whether by car, coach or bus, visitors will find Newquay one of the best motoring centres in Cornwall. It is well placed for drives to all parts of the Duchy, the roads are good, the town boasts efficient garages, and there is a good network of public road services serving all places of interest.

Here, then, is a holiday playground ready-made by Nature. No man-made pier can compare in grandeur with Newquay's natural pier, Towan Head, which runs for nearly a mile out to sea, covered with soft, springy turf and gay with thrift and other sea flowers. The extremity is a chaos of rocks against which the waves of the Atlantic hurl themselves with stupendous power—in rough weather a sight to be remembered.

From this point the sweep of the coast-line can be followed round, the sheer perpendicular cliffs and rocks showing more or less prominently above the belts of yellow sand, north-eastward past Porth and Watergate Bay to Bedruthan Steps, to Park Head, and on till Trevose Head, with its lighthouse, limits the vision.

On either side of the Headland is a fine bay, that to the east being the larger and more populous, though an increasing number of visitors favour the more open Fistral Bay, west of the Headland. Newquay can offer shelter from almost any wind that blows, unless it comes from the north-east.

At first sight the town appears to consist of a long, winding and busy street close to the edge of the cliffs, with houses and shops on each side. Between the buildings occasional glimpses of the sea can be obtained, and by turning out of the main street, terraces and slopes facing the beaches can be reached in a minute. Large numbers of new houses have been built in recent years on the higher ground away from the cliffs, and though these are farther from the sea they have a remarkable range of coast views. The town has also extended southwards on the other side of the golf links towards East Pentire Point, while eastwards it is difficult to see where Newquay ends and Porth begins. The most prominent building in the town is the **Church of St Michael,** well situated on the slope of Mount Wise.

The Beaches. Newquay's eastern bay is lined with a series of smaller bays. These are floored with firm sand and are ideal for bathing. Immediately east of the Harbour and overlooked by the Camelot Cinema is **Towan Beach.**

North-eastward of Towan Beach is the **Great Western,** or

Bothwicks Beach, which can be reached at low tide by going round the **Island.** There are good changing facilities. At high tide access to this beach is obtained by the winding road by the Great Western Hotel.

The next beach north-eastward again is the **Tolcarne Beach.** This is reached from the others at low tide, by steps from Narrowcliff at high water and by a cliff path at Crigga Head. Here again is a plentiful supply of huts. **Crigga** and **Lusty Glaze** beaches are still farther on, and can easily be reached at low water. From the latter there is a path to the top, coming out on the road to Glendorgal and Porth. *In all cases the tide must be watched, especially when caverns are being explored.* Beyond Lusty Glaze are **Porth, Whipsiderry** and **Watergate** beaches.

Westward of the Headland is **Fistral Bay** with a splendid stretch of sands. With the golf links at the back and splendid views of the Towan Headland and Pentire to north and west respectively, it is not surprising that this western bay is becoming more popular every year, though extreme care is necessary when bathing.

The **Harbour** is merely a little cove guarded by two very solid stone piers. Access is by a long flight of stone steps or by a rather steep road leading down to the harbour. This rocky inlet, with its sandy floor at low water, is charming, and is increasingly popular with children. Bathing is allowed. Around it are perpendicular cliffs smothered, in season, with wall-flowers and valerian from base to summit, and rich always with ferns and flowers—a rare and lovely picture. There are the occasional fishing boats (bearing the distinctive PW of Padstow, the port of registration), but principally yachts, and motor and rowing boats, the majority of which are available for hire.

To reach the North Quay, continue northwards along Fore Street until North Quay Hill is reached on the right. A few yards down the hill are seats from which a grand panoramic view of Newquay's magnificent beaches is obtained, with the busy little harbour just below.

Following the coast towards the Headland, the War Memorial comes into sight, and then **Towan Headland,** or rather the final portion of it. The highest part is the extreme end where the waves make fine play over the rocks at the base.

Fistral Bay on the western side has a fine sweeping expanse of sand. The Atlantic rollers here are excellent for surf-riding. *There is a flag-warning system in operation.*

The large detached rock close to the Point is the Goose Rock. A cliff pathway extends round Fistral Bay, from the Life-boat House, skirting the golf links and joining the Esplanade Road which is a continuation of Mount Wise. The turf-covered Point, or **Pentire Headland,** as it is properly called, is a place to be visited. The Newquay Council have bought it and so preserved it for public use. The views are magnificent.

The end of Pentire Point adjoining the golf links is fast developing into a popular suburb with a number of admirably situated hotels, and buses that connect the Point with the town and railway station. In spite of development however, two historic tumuli are preserved at the end of Pentire Avenue.

These Pentire Points east and west of the Gannel estuary must not be confused with the more massive Pentire Point guarding the entrance to the Camel at Padstow 20 miles farther up the coast.

Cliffs and Caves. Newquay may have no 'Front' in the ordinary sense of that word, but a walk along the firm sands north-eastwards from the Harbour affords a splendid view of the fine cliffs upon which the town has grown. When the tide is out it is possible to walk all the way to Porth. Immediately on setting out attention is claimed by the lofty detached piece of cliff known as the **Island,** joined to the mainland by a light suspension bridge. All around are piles of jagged rocks, and here and there will be seen small wave-worn caves. Overlooking the Island and Towan Beach is **Killacourt,** with putting greens, and steps down to the Towan Beach. The cave under Tolcarne Head shows some fine colouring. Across the wide beach is the **Bishop's Cave,** at the foot of Crigga Point, with a grand entrance, and a passage called the Creeping Hole through to another cave. From here onwards to Porth the masses of rock are very fine, and appear much more imposing when closely viewed than when seen from the cliffs above.

Above Crigga and bordering Narrowcliff, opposite the Astor Cinema, are the **Barrowfields,** purchased by the town as an open space. Here may be seen some burial grounds or barrows of the Bronze Age (2500–1800 B.C.).

The **Trenance Valley** is the most sheltered part of Newquay. Open to the south and west and screened from northerly winds by the high ground on which the town has been built, its lovely **Gardens** are a glorious mass of colour in late spring and summer. It may be reached by the steep Trenance Road, or by Tolcarne Road, Ulalia Road or Edgcumbe Avenue. In this delightful vale Newquay has a second climate, and here invalids can always take needful outdoor exercise or sit enjoying the surroundings. North-east of the fine viaduct which carries the railway over the valley are the sports grounds, with tennis courts, bowling greens, and putting greens, a car park and a large pavilion where teas, etc., are provided. South of the viaduct are beautiful **Public Gardens** (mentioned above) with seats, shelters, shady walks, a stream, and a pleasant **Boating Lake.** Nearby is **Newquay Zoo** (*daily 10–dusk*). The gardens and lake are a Bird Sanctuary. The broad road between the Viaduct and **Trevemper Bridge** over the **Gannel Estuary** runs beside the old bridge—an interesting memorial of days past.

Excursions from Newquay

I. To Porth and St Columb Minor

Porth lies 1 mile northward on the coast. The extreme point of Porth Island is Trevelgue Head beneath which are the Mermaid's Cave and the Blowing Hole, which run right through the rock. For the **Porth Caves** return from the island, cross the bridge and turn to the left to rock steps leading down to the small rocky beach. The caves are interesting and have fanciful names—Banqueting Hall, Cathedral Cavern, Infernal Regions, Fern Cavern and Boulder Cavern.

St Columb Minor (*Cross Mount*) is a fast-developing village on the St Columb Major road. The church has a notable tower, the second highest in Cornwall, and inside is some fourteenth-century work of some interest.

The picturesque **Porth Valley** lies beyond St Columb Minor, and a short distance to the eastward is **Rialton** (the *Reiltone* of Domesday), at one time the summer residence of Prior Vivian, the last Prior of Bodmin. What remains is a beautiful low house, the old Hall being divided into two storeys, but still with decorated wagon-roof. There is a tunnel-vaulted porch on the ground floor. In the courtyard, now a garden, is a small Holy Well visible from the main road. This house is only occasionally shown to visitors by special favour. At Rialton farm to the south is to be seen, built into the wall of a barn, an inscribed stone of the fifth century. Still farther eastward is **St Pedyr's Well,** reached through Treloy Farm, and on the south side of the valley, but better reached by motorists by a turning to the left on the Indian Queens road 1½ miles beyond the Quintrel Downs cross-roads, is **Colan.** The road is narrow, steep and rather swampy in bad weather, but clearly marked. The lonely little church, built about 1300, consists of a chancel and nave of five bays, aisle and south transept, south porch and tower. The base of the old rood screen and stairway remain.

II. To the Gannel and Crantock

The River Gannel can be crossed by a small plank bridge at half ebb-tide, and the passage remains open until $2\frac{1}{2}$ hours before high water. There is no regular ferry, but the boatmen will generally put people across for a small fee. Otherwise Trevemper Bridge ($1\frac{3}{4}$ miles inland) must be used.

An alternative way is to take the bus to Pentire, walk down through Fern Pit Gardens and cross by Fern Pit ferry. The ferry runs all day in summer.

On the opposite side of the estuary is the pretty, wooded **Penpol Creek.** Except at lowest ebb it is well to resist temptations to make short cuts, and to cross the creek by the plank bridge at its head. Then ascend a steep lane, bear to the left, and shortly take a field path on the right. The path rejoins the lane which soon leads to Crantock.

Crantock is a place to examine at leisure. Note, for example, a farm building on the left as the village is entered from Penpol: the lintel of its door is formed from an old carved figurehead. The church is most interesting. St Carantoc founded an oratory here in the fifth century. A collegiate church of considerable importance existed for centuries, being founded early in the thirteenth century by Bishop Bruere. The choir was reconstructed in 1224 and a tower added. In 1337 Bishop Bantingham called attention to the perilous state of the tower and left money for its completion, but in 1412 it fell upon the nave and reduced it to ruins. Rebuilding was undertaken shortly afterwards. A further restoration was carried out in the nineteenth century. The interior is dark, but as the eye accustoms itself the full beauty of the very fine screen, incorporating portions of the original, can be appreciated. Much of the fourteenth-century parclose screen in the south chapel is also original. Note the modern bench-ends and a number of beautiful stained-glass windows. The font, of native elvan, is inscribed with the date 1474, but is probably of Norman origin, the date commemorating rebuilding after the fall of the tower. It is said that the foundations of the church are pre-conquest, but the earliest visible features are Norman choir arches. The chancel arch is Early English, as is also the western tower, as high as the belfry.

From Crantock a pleasant walk or drive leads to **West Pentire,** with hotel, car park, and tea gardens within easy reach of **Porth** or **Polly Joke** (*see* p. 55) and Crantock Beach.

The **Gannel Estuary** is very picturesque, but is often overlooked by Newquay visitors because it is slightly off the beaten track. At low water on the Crantock side it is possible to walk seawards along the sands from the Gannel crossing to the mouth, which is nearly a mile wide, guarded on the right and left respectively by East and West Pentire Points. If the tide is flowing instead of ebbing, the water should be carefully noted, as it rises fairly quickly and the sands are sometimes spongy and dangerous. (On no account should an attempt be made to wade *across* the estuary until the advice of local boatmen has been sought as to tide, route, conditions of sand, and so on.) It is a pleasant walk by this route to Crantock, either by the sands or the field path which follows the coast. Entering Crantock Bay, the views are magnificent. Here the road runs by the side of the stream to the village.

A convenient way of seeing the Gannel is to take a bus or the cliff path from Newquay, by the side of the golf links, and continue all the way round Fistral Bay to East Pentire Point. Part of the journey is along the high ground of the promontory, with the sea on one side and the Gannel on the other. Returning, continue up the valley to the old mill, and back to the town by way of the main road, passing Trenance Gardens and the Viaduct.

III. To Trerice Manor and St Newlyn East

Trerice Manor (*April to October, daily 11–1, 2–6; charge*), a National Trust property, is best visited on the way to St Newlyn East by going via St Columb Minor to Quintrel Downs and then a mile farther on, turning off to the right at Kestle Mill. Though dating in part from the fourteenth century, Trerice is essentially a sixteenth-century manor house. The dates 1572 and 1578 are virtually the last touches added to the house. The plaster ceilings of the two large apartments are magnificent. They were carried out by Sir John Arundell, Admiral to Queen Elizabeth I. The large hall window contains 576 panes of glass.

St Newlyn East, 2 miles beyond Trerice, has a good example of one of the larger Cornish parish churches. This fifteenth-century building, dedicated to St Newlina, a sixth-century missionary, has an interesting Norman font carved with lilies and cats, some fifteenth-century carved oak bench-ends, a well-preserved Royal Arms of Charles I, and a handsome screen and choir stalls added in the restoration of 1883. Of interest outside is the fig tree growing out of the wall some 6 feet above ground.

IV. To St Mawgan and Carnanton Woods

Leave Newquay by the B3276 passing through Porth and reaching the magnificent sands at **Watergate,** a deep cleft between hills. Here there is a choice of roads. Either take the very steep hill beside the hotel to Trevarrian or continue along the B3276, an easier but longer route.

Mawgan Porth, with its high rocky cliffs, is very popular. Its breakers provide fine sport for surfing. Here the luxuriant Vale of Lanherne opens to the sea and a glorious stretch of sand is available at low tide.

The inland road from Mawgan Porth through the hamlet of Gluvian leads to **St Mawgan** village charmingly set among trees. The River Menalhyl runs down the valley and with the church makes a delightful picture. St Mawgan's beauty has a wide reputation and it is popular with artists as well as with campers and caravanners.

St Mawgan Church, with its fine tower and interesting crosses, is one of the most picturesque in the county. The nave, chancel with hagioscope and north transept are of the thirteenth century, as is also the lower part of the tower. The medieval font, dating from 1100, has a red painted bowl, and stands on modern Devon marble columns. The fine old pulpit dates from 1553, and the beautiful open screen, with delicate painted pillars, though much restored, is of the fifteenth century.

The Carmelite nunnery adjoining the church was the old manor house of the Arundell family. The chapel is open and services are held on Sundays.

The entrance to **Carnanton Woods** is 100 yards up the hill from the *Falcon Inn.* A new road leads through the woods to First Lodge on the St Columb Major road. The ferns are magnificent and the views very fine.

V. To Cubert and Holywell

The **Holy Well** is about 2 miles from the church in a north-westerly direction. It is in a cave, access to which can be had at low water during neap tides, but during spring tides it may be reached soon after ebbing half-tide. A series of rock basins like natural holy-water stoups lead up to the well, which is larger than the rest. Note the curious pinnacle of rock on the beach of Holywell Bay. The cleft rock off the head is Carter's or Gull Rocks.

On the coast $\frac{1}{2}$ mile north of the Holy Well is **Porth** or **Polly Joke,** a picturesque V-shaped beach between the cliffs, fed by a stream. The distance from Newquay is $3\frac{1}{2}$ miles. The origin of the curious name is obscure, but in Cornish it means 'Beach of the Jackdaws (chogha)'. The return to Newquay may be made via Crantock.

VI. To St Columb Major

Leave Newquay by the A3059 which leads in 7 miles to St Columb Major. The predominance of slate and grey stone in its buildings gives it a somewhat bleak appearance; but from its lofty situation it overlooks some very attractive country and the road from Newquay via St Columb Minor is most delightful.

The ancient Cornish hurling game is played here twice a year (Shrove Tuesday and Saturday week following) and shows no signs of decadence. Of particular historical interest is the *St Columb Green Book* (so called from its binding), preserving the Churchwardens' Accounts from the days of Elizabeth I. In 1593 there is mention of payment of 10s. for a silver ball for the hurling.

The **Church** (dedicated to St Columba, an Irish saint) has much of interest. The fine tower rises from outside the building, and rests on two arches, with passage beneath. The chancel has a beautifully carved roof and the modern oak screens are very fine.

About 2¼ miles east by south of St Columb Major, but a mile farther by road, is **Castle-an-Dinas,** important remains of an early British encampment. The hill itself is called Castle Downs and rises 703 feet. There are two tumuli within the enclosure.

Nearly 3 miles on the Wadebridge road are the **Nine Maidens,** a group of upright stones said to date from 1500 BC.

VII. To the Roche Rocks

Leave Newquay by the A392 and in 8 miles at the Indian Queens cross-roads turn left along the A30 Bodmin road. In about 4 miles turn left along the B3274 for Roche. This district is one of open expanses of bog and rough grass, dotted with old workings and crossed by rough stone walls. To the south-east rise the enormous white pyramids of the St Austell china clay pits.

The **Roche Rocks** rise spectacularly a hundred feet from the plain and are surmounted by the picturesque remains of the chapel of St Michael, licensed in 1409, and a hermit's cell. The chapel perched on the tallest rock was 22 feet 6 inches long by 10 feet 6 inches wide. It is possible to reach the hermit's cell by the vertical iron ladder on the south side and a second ladder ascends to the chapel.

The village of **Roche,** close to the rocks, has a church with a beautiful Norman font and an interesting cross in the churchyard with rude ornamentation on each side of the shaft and four little holes in the head.

Newquay to St Ives

The A3075 runs southward to join the A30 Land's End road about 5.
miles north of Redruth. But it is well worth making the diversion to
visit Perranporth and St Agnes. Leave Newquay by the A3075 and in
about 7 miles turn right along the B3285 to—

Perranporth

Bathing Excellent, some of the best surf
bathing in England. Firm sands extend
for about 3 miles at low tide when
bathing is unwise.
Bowls In Boscawen Garden.
Distances Crantock, 6 miles; London,
258; Newquay, 9; St Agnes, 4; Truro, 9.

Early Closing Wednesday.
Gliding At Trevellas Airfield, ½ mile
along the St Agnes road.
Golf Course on the cliffs to the east.
Tennis Perranporth Lawn Tennis Club
open to visitors.

Perranporth has long been noted for its fine rock scenery and its magnificent expanse of hard, golden sand. The town lies at the point where
two lovely valleys open on to a broad expanse of sand—a children's paradise.

At first glance, Perranporth appears to be an odd mixture of the old
and the new—with an undeveloped site here and there. The business
quarter is pleasantly situated overlooking the well-stocked, colourful
Boscawen Public Gardens, the model yacht pond and boating lake for
children. But the main attraction here is the magnificent beach of firm,
clean sand which, at low tide, extends nearly 3 miles between Droskyn
Point and Ligger Point. Perranporth is noted for its surf riding. The
district is wild and romantic and the pure Atlantic breezes exceptionally
healthy and invigorating. The coast scenery is varied. To the north are
the vast sandy towans rolling towards Holywell Bay: to the south, the
towering rugged cliffs of **Droskyn Point,** with their attractive rock
archways, caves and pools. Not all these arches are natural formations,
although the sea has modified their original shape. Some are disused

mine workings, cut in the sixteenth and seventeenth centuries in the course of exploiting the Droskyn Lode of tin, copper, and silver-bearing lead ores.

To St Piran's Lost Church. Follow the Newquay road (passing the post office), climbing steeply past golf links. In just over 1 mile, where the main road bends sharply to the right, keep straight on (past some cottages on left) along a lane for half a mile until, facing the next turn on right, a white gate—the Gear Gate—is seen in the wall on the left. Pass through the gate (no fee), and follow the track marked by white painted stones; short cuts are obvious here and there.

Legend declares that **St Piran** floated over from Ireland on a mill-stone—a story possibly arising from the fact that he brought over an altar-stone (the ancient Irish altar stones were like miniature millstones in shape). He arrived in Cornwall about 500, and built a church close to the spot where he landed. This church had to be abandoned in the eleventh century as the sand overcame it. A new church was built further inland which was frequently threatened with the same fate, but its excavations may now be seen.

St Piran's Round lies about 30 yards north of the Newquay road near Rose, 1 mile east of Perranporth. Scheduled as an ancient monument, it is a more or less natural amphitheatre 130 feet in diameter and capable of accommodating 2,000 people. In it were performed the Cornish miracle plays.

From Perranporth the B3285 road runs south for 4½ miles to—

St Agnes and Trevaunance Cove

Bathing Very good, from fine clean sand. Surfing popular.
Distances Falmouth, 15 miles; London, 261; Newquay, 12; Redruth, 7; St Ives, 19.

Early Closing Wednesday.
Hotels *Rose-in-Vale, Rosemundy House.*
Population 4,747.

To those who delight in glorious seascapes, high, open moorland plentifully dappled with sea-pinks, gorse and heather, with intersecting valleys and streams leading down to the sea, St Agnes has much to offer. It is a healthy little town. The air is superb, the blend of pure, bracing Atlantic breezes with soft moorland air having a rare tonic effect.

Probably the greatest charm of St Agnes lies in the infinite variety and beauty of its immediate surroundings. The town is built high up on the slopes of a hill and the scene changes every few yards as new and delightful vistas open up.

St Agnes is the home of the **Cornish Seal Sanctuary** which cares for baby seals which are injured or washed up on shore, eventually returning them to the sea.

The **Model Village** (*April to October, daily 10–10; charge*) is built to exact scale and in the same materials as the actual buildings. Included are miniature versions of Truro Cathedral and Restormel Castle.

The parish church of St Agnes was rebuilt over 100 years ago. Unlike most Cornish churches, it boasts both a tower and a spire.

The famous artist John Opie was born at St Agnes, in 1761.

St Agnes is bigger than appears at first sight. It meanders in all directions and the parish embraces **Chapel Porth** and **Porthtowan** on the south-west and **Blue Hills Mine** (where the famous Easter Saturday Hill Climb is held), **Trevellas, Trevellas Porth** and most of **Trevellas Airfield** (famous Fighter Station in World War II and now a popular gliding venue) on the north-east; to the south—**Mount Hawke** and **Blackwater;** and to the east, the hamlet of **Mithian.** The whole district abounds in beautiful walks and rambles.

The adjacent **Trevaunance Cove** is without doubt one of the most lovely natural rocky inlets to be found anywhere round the coast.

On a sunny morning, with a few clouds, the colour of the sea here is truly magnificent and worth travelling a very long way to enjoy. Almost every conceivable shade of blue, green and purple mingle to delight the eye. The effect of vivid colouring is further enhanced by the rich buffs and browns of the great rocky headlands which rise steeply from the sea on either side.

Below high-water mark the beach is of firm, clean sand. Bathing, particularly surf-riding, is excellent. But, as with all rocky coasts, it is definitely dangerous to swim out to sea, especially at low water or on an ebb tide.

St Agnes Beacon. The town is flanked on the south-west by St Agnes Beacon (630 feet N.T.), a prominent land and seamark for many miles around. The ascent is quite easy at one or two points and will well repay the effort for the extensive views in all directions. On a clear day it is possible to pick out over 30 church towers from the summit; to look across south-eastwards into Falmouth Harbour and south-westwards to St Michael's Mount. Inland, the 'Cornish Giants,' Brown

Willy (1,375 feet) and Rough Tor (1,312 feet), approximately 40 miles distant as the crow flies, can be seen under favourable conditions.

Chapel Porth, a miniature rocky cove about 2 miles south-westward, is a favourite walk over the cliffs, or may be reached by car in a little over a mile from the Goonvrea side of Beacon Drive. The road is steep in parts, narrow and rough and ends at the car park and café adjoining the beach. At low tide there is an excellent sandy beach and there are many fine caves. It is National Trust property and an ideal spot for a quiet rest.

The best route to take from St Agnes is the road to **Porthtowan** with its lofty cliffs and broad sands. Then continue until you join the B3300 which leads to the small resort of **Portreath,** which was once a port serving the mines round Camborne but is now known for its glorious sandy beach and fine surfing.

The coast road continues over the heather-clad cliffs to **Gwithian.** The route passes Deadman's Cove and Hell's Mouth and there are fine views of jagged rocks with the waves creaming at their feet. After Gwithian the road heads inland to join the main Land's End road at Hayle.

Back on the A30 and reached from Portreath by the B3300, are the twin towns of Redruth and Camborne with a combined population of more than 27,000.

Redruth clings to the sides of two steep hills, a crowded, somewhat old-fashioned town with modern additions and amenities. The town is both an important commercial shopping centre and an excellent base for touring. Friday is the local market day. At one time Redruth was the old mining capital of Cornwall and had associations with John Wesley and George Fox, the founder of the Society of Friends. William Murdock, a Scottish engineer, invented gas lighting and the cottage and shop where he made experiments leading to the discovery is still to be seen in Cross Street, where a tablet records the event of 1792.

On the left of the road when leaving Redruth in the direction of Camborne is the wild, rugged hill known as **Carn Brea.** The hill is chiefly granite, 750 feet high, and was probably a military station in Neolithic times. It presents some magnificent views.

Beside the A30 at Pool between the twin towns may be seen the **East Pool Winding Engine** (*daily 11–1, 2–6; charge*). Owned by the National Trust, it is the only complete surviving example of the winding engines that pumped water and wound cages in the tin mines. Visitors can see the machinery in motion and tour the building. On the Portreath road the **Tolgus Tin Stream Museum** (*March to November, daily 10–*

6 ; *charge*) is part of the only surviving tin stream works and retains the original water wheels.

Although in no sense one of Cornwall's holiday resorts, **Camborne** is an interesting place and one of the few big industrial centres near the north coast of the Duchy. It is a busy and pleasant town in spite of the proximity of several important and well-known engineering and other industrial undertakings. Apart from its busy industries Camborne is the shopping centre for the scattered rural districts of which it is the hub.

Richard Trevithick, who invented the high-pressure steam engine was born close by, at Poole. There is a fine statue of Trevithick fronting the Passmore Edwards Library. One of the more important buildings is the **School of Mines** where those making mining their career receive valuable instruction. Owing to the decline of the mining industry in Cornwall most graduates take up positions overseas. The **Holman Mining Museum** (*Monday to Friday 9–12, 1–4.30*) houses models, machines and documents relating to two hundred years of Cornish mining.

Follow the A30 for 8 miles from Camborne to join the road from Gwithian and arrive in **Hayle.** This is a straggly place with huge towans along the shore. It was once an important port for the tin-mining industry and some raw materials are still imported by sea by local industrial firms. At **Bird Paradise** (*daily 10–dusk ; charge*) more than 120 species of rare and beautiful birds may be seen in 7 acres of grounds and there is also a children's zoo. The road follows the eastern bank of the Hayle estuary until a right fork is taken along the A3074 which leads through Lelant and Carbis Bay to—

St Ives

Bathing Beaches of firm golden sand. There is a beautiful stretch of sand from Lelant to Carrack Dhu. Surfing from Porthmeor Beach.

Bowls Public green on the edge of the cliff overlooking Porthmeor Beach. The greens of the St Ives Bowling Club are in the Belyars and are open to visitors.

Buses Buses run from the Malakoff to Penzance via Carbis Bay, Lelant and St Erth; to Penzance via Nancledra, Ludgvan and Castle Gate; to Land's End via Zennor.

Cinemas *Royal* in Royal Square; *Scala* in High Street.

Distances Camborne, 13 miles; Falmouth, 25; Land's End, 22; Lizard, 26; London, 279; Newquay, 35; Penzance, 9; Truro, 23.

Early Closing Thursday.

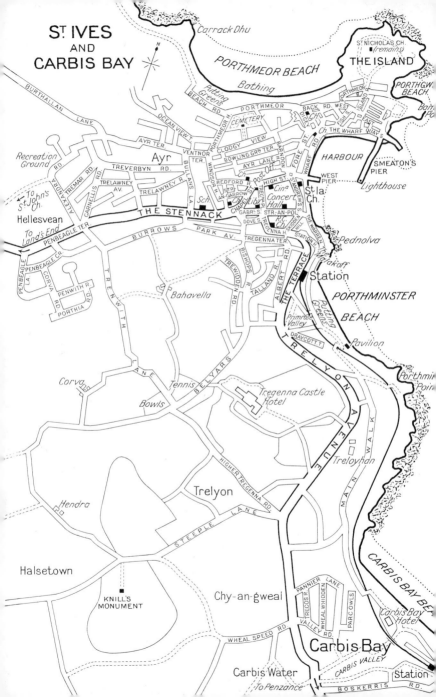

Entertainments Plays, musical recitals, concerts and ballet are presented at the Concert Hall in the Guildhall.
Golf *West Cornwall Golf Club*, Lelant.
Hotels *Boskerris*, Carbis Bay; *Carbis*, Carbis Bay; *Chy-an-Albany; Chy-an-Dour; Chy-an-Drea; Chy-Morvah; Garrack; Hendra's*, Carbis Bay; *Karenza*, Carbis Bay; *Master Roberts; Pedn-Olva;*

Porthminster; St Ives Bay; St Margarets, Carbis Bay; *St Uny*, Carbis Bay; *Tregenna Castle; Western.*
Population 9,760.
Library Gabriel Street.
Tennis Porthmeor Beach; Tregenna Castle Hotel.
Tourist Information Centre Gabriel Street.

St Ives is a place for idlers rather than whirlwind travellers. The miles of beautiful sands and safe bathing beaches, abundant fishing facilities, a fascinating harbour, fine coast and wooded slopes, make it a paradise for young and old.

For a century, St Ives has been the mecca of artists and of those who appreciate beauty of colour and form. The clear light, the wonderful, ever-changing hues of the sea, the colourful boats, the picturesque old houses and artists' studios, have attracted countless artists. Through their paintings, exhibited throughout the world, St Ives has become a familiar place to people of many nations.

One of the most famous of the artists who made their home at St Ives was Barbara Hepworth who bequeathed some of her finest sculptures to the **Barbara Hepworth Museum** (*Monday to Saturday 10–5*).

Close to the bus and railway stations is the open space known as the **Malakoff,** from which trees and walls on the right fall away to give lovely views over the harbour, the church tower, the Island and Porthminster Beach.

From the Malakoff, the main road runs steeply into the town, via Tregenna Hill to the **Public Library.** Tregenna Hill leads to **Tregenna Place,** on the right of which is **Street-an-Pol.** Here is the attractive flower-decked Guildhall with a fine Concert Room and dance floor.

At the foot of Tregenna Place is the **Head Post Office** where turn right along the High Street for the **Parish Church** and the **Harbour.** At the western end of the harbour, near the steps leading to Porthgwidden Beach, is Wheal Dream in which is the **Town Museum** (*June to September, Monday to Friday 10.30–12.30, 2.30–5*) with its many relics of the town and neighbourhood, and some pictures.

The old town, with its winding streets, its church, and ancient houses, clusters round the harbour and behind it and on either side rise hills which are being covered with houses favoured by visitors. These houses command sweeping views of the harbour and its many activities, and of the great bay from the Island to Godrevy Point, on the north-east, where at night the lighthouse sheds its beams. It is about 4 miles from point to point across the bay, the old town of St Ives being huddled on the eastern side of the neck of land of which the Island is the end, and spreading itself on the shore of the mainland in a south-easterly direction towards Carbis Bay, and westward towards the heathery downs towards Clodgy Point. Old St Ives, in fact, is now enclosed by considerable and very attractive residential areas, with ample modern hotel and other accommodation for visitors, and those who expect to find merely the picturesque old fishing town will be surprised at the extent to which St Ives has grown in recent years.

The **Parish Church** dates from 1410 to 1426 and is said to have been erected on the site of a Norman Church. It is dedicated to St Ia (or Eia), one of the lady missionaries from Ireland who landed here between 450 and 500. She built an oratory on or near to the present site. The lofty tower of the church, 119 feet, is the chief architectural feature in any general view of the town. Of interest are the wagon roof and the many fine carvings, some of which date from the fifteenth century. There are some good windows especially either side of the south door. Outside against this door is a fine fifteenth-century cross, 12 feet high.

The Harbour is much more than a sheltering-place for boats. At St Ives one goes down to the Harbour almost as to a club, for since everybody drifts down there sooner or later one is sure to meet friends. From the north pier there is a magnificent view along many miles of the rugged north coast from the Hayle estuary, past Godrevy Lighthouse, St Agnes Beacon, and far beyond to Trevose Head near Padstow. At all times the Harbour is a miracle of colour—the boats, the water, the wooded cliffs and many-tinted houses and beyond them gleaming golden sands. The lighthouse half-way along the Pier was formerly at the end. It was erected by Smeaton, the builder of the old Eddystone Lighthouse. Between the two piers by which the harbour is protected is the Fisherman's Chapel, and near the parish church is the **Lifeboat House.** It was in 1840 that the first lifeboat was placed at St Ives (the Institutions had then been in existence only sixteen years) since when over 650 lives have been saved.

Westward of the Harbour is the oldest and quaintest part of the town. Running northward from the church is Fore Street in which stands the **Barnes Museum of Cinematography** (*daily 11–1, 2.30–5*). From Fore Street the **Digey** goes off to the left and has on its left side Hick's

Court, in which is a carved archway. By going under it and then turning to the right a characteristic part of the town is seen. Returning to the Digey and following it northward (leftward) one arrives at **Porthmeor Beach,** a fine sandy bay, splendid for surf-bathing. Beyond it are putting greens. To the left, at the extremity of the bay, is the headland of **Carrack Dhu.**

One can return by Back Road, wander about the quaintest of little streets and go by Island Road to the **Island** originally doubtless an island in fact as in name. Then sand accumulated and formed the present causeway, now chequered with narrow lanes and strange houses, known by outlandish names. From the crest of the Island views are obtained of the bay, and of the coastline to the west, broken here and there by headlands, the best known of which are **Man's Head** and **Clodgy Point,** the latter a favourite picnicking spot. On the top of the Island is a stone building which marked the site of **St Nicholas Chapel,** an old shrine of St Ia, pulled down by the War Office in 1904. To the east of the Island is **Porthgwidden Beach,** a favourite spot for children. The grass-covered headland is sometimes black with the nets of fishermen, stretched out to dry. The comparatively flat ground between the Island and the town is a car park, almost at sea-level.

Carbis Bay

Carbis Bay lies to the south-east and is part of the great bay of St Ives. Only 1¼ miles separate it from the town, and between the two places cliff walks meander along the coast, crossing and re-crossing the railway by light bridges. At one time Carbis Bay was known only as a picnicking haunt, but of late years it has attracted a considerable number of residents and visitors.

There is good bathing on excellent sands, boating and fishing. Nearby are the famed Lelant golf links. The long line of cliffs is broken by a tree-clad gorge, where the tea gardens are popular. Across the bay is Godrevy Lighthouse.

There is a fine walk between St Ives and Carbis Bay along the coast, passing, high up above Porthminster Point, the house where the 'huer' watched for the first signs of pilchards in the Bay, in the days when they were caught by means of seine nets. On all the headlands around west Cornwall men called huers, from the French word meaning 'to shout', watched during the season for the purple tinge on the sea that told of the presence of a shoal of fish. When the anxiously awaited sign was discovered, the huers cried 'heva', 'heva' (found, found), and away went the seine boats, the course taken by the crews being directed by the watchers who bawled instructions through trumpets and waved 'bushes', the name given to rough wooden frames covered with calico.

Excursions from St Ives

I. To Clodgy Point

West of the Island a footpath skirts Porthmeor Beach to Carthew Point. A short distance beyond is **Clodgy Point,** from which may be viewed a vast expanse of sea and coastline. Northeastward across St Ives Bay the prospect includes Godrevy Island and Lighthouse at the extremity of the inlet; beyond them St Agnes Beacon, and still further Trevose Head, stretching out into the sea some dozen miles north of Newquay. Southwestward from Clodgy the coast shows five headlands descending steeply into the sea.

Good walkers may make the excursion circular by taking the delightful cliff walk past the Five Points to the cove and cliffs at Treveal, a picnic resort some 2½ miles distant, and returning to St Ives by a footpath passing through Trevalgan and Trowan and about 2 miles from Treveal striking the lane between Clodgy and St Ives. Or from Treveal one can strike southward to the Zennor–St Ives road, along which buses run.

II. To Lelant and St Erth

By foot follow the lovely Hain cliff walk to Carbis Bay and then over the golf links to the point where the land is broken by the River Hayle. It is also possible to walk along the shore, making use of steps at a few points when the tide is high. From the mouth of the estuary it is 10 minutes' walk to Lelant.

By road **Lelant** lies 3 miles from St Ives on the A3074. The parish is one of the many in Cornwall which have suffered from accumulations of sand. There is a tradition that where the church now stands a whole town was overwhelmed by sand and finally lost. Little more than a century ago the church, which is ½ mile from the village, was itself in danger of being buried, but the marram grass which was planted around it has checked the encroachment. The principal features of interest are the panelled roof of the chancel, the Norman arch and pillars (restored) and Norman capitals, the carved roof of the south aisle, the staircase to a rood screen in the north wall, the Norman font, and the monuments at the west end of the south side.

A more recent attraction is **Lelant Model Village** (*open daily*, *charge*), which includes a scale-model village, water gardens and museum.

Shortly after Lelant turn right along the A30 and in about ½ mile at St Erth station turn left for **St Erth.** The church was built in the fourteenth century, repaired in 1742 and restored in 1872. The fourteenth-century tower consists of three stages and has battlements and pinnacles. Gargoyles halfway up the tower form the most interesting external feature, as no other church in West Cornwall has such figures. Internally the church is notable for the woodwork of the wagon roof with its magnificent carving and floral bosses. The churchyard contains interesting old crosses. Near the church is a small, low, three-arched bridge, spanning the Hayle. Leland, the antiquary (1506–52), speaks of the bridge being two hundred years old in *his* time. The village has some picturesque houses and attractive doorways.

III. To Trencrom Hill
Trencrom Hill lies about 3½ miles south of St Ives. It may be reached by footpaths from Carbis Bay via Trevarrack. By car the easiest route is to follow the B3311 Penzance road from St Ives, turn left in about 2½ miles to Brunnion and then keep left for the hill. On the summit are remains of an ancient camp believed to date from the Iron Age. The hill, 550 feet above sea-level, is a fine point of vantage for views of the surrounding country. Among the most prominent features of the extensive prospect are St Ives Bay and Godrevy Point on the north; St Michael's Mount and the Lizard on the south; Hayle and the Hayle estuary on the east, and at the foot of the hill Trevethoe Park.

St Ives to Land's End and Penzance

Leave St Ives by the B3311 and in a mile keep right along the B3306 Land's End road, which leads in a further 4 miles to **Zennor.** The village is dominated by its church with a square pinnacled tower. It has a four-teenth-century font, an Early English window and a carved bench-end on which hangs a tale. It represents the traditional mermaid of Zennor who is said to have visited the church to hear the marvellous singing of the squire's son, and enticed him to return with her to the sea.

Opposite the church is the **Tinners' Arms Inn,** a reminder that tin mining once flourished here.

The **Wayside Museum** (*Whitsun to October, daily*) houses an inter-esting collection of agricultural, mining and domestic tools and imple-ments, including some working models. There is also an archaeological collection relating to West Cornwall.

One of the sights of the village is the **Giant's Rock,** or Logan Stone, on the seaward side of the Church. Follow the lane leading north-west from the church and the stone will be seen in fields on the right directly one is clear of buildings. The rock was at one time very sensitive, and legend has it that one way of becoming a witch was to climb on the Giant's Rock nine times without shaking it. **Zennor Quoit** is also worth seeing. There are many cromlechs in Cornwall, but that at Zennor is remarkable in being the only one that contains two sepulchres covered by one great stone, the largest of the kind in England. The slab, 18 feet by 9½ feet, was formerly supported by seven upright stones. The crom-lech is a mile eastward of the village, on the inland side of the main road.

Gurnard's Head. A short distance out of Zennor, a path to the right leads to the Gurnard's Head, a narrow promontory running out due north from the mainland. It is one of the wildest and grandest headlands in the country, once known as Treryn Dinas, for it was one of Cornwall's famous cliff castles. On the isthmus there are still remains of the fortifi-cations. From its situation, which resembles that of its namesake on the coast south-west of Penzance, the castle must have been of great strength. As a point of vantage from which to view this portion of the romantic coast of Cornwall, Gurnard's Head is unexcelled. It is a place to visit and revisit, in calm and in storm.

The deep cove, ¾ mile westward of the Head, is **Porthmeor,** at the head of which slate gives place to granite. The hamlet, which is about ½ mile inland, can be reached directly from Gurnard's Head or *via* Trereen and the high road. At Porthmeor a fortified village of the Iron Age (100 B.C.–A.D. 200), has been excavated. About ½ mile farther along the high road and just north of it is **Bosigran.** The head of its promontory, ½ mile away, formed a cliff castle 400 feet above the sea. Between Bosigran Castle and Morvah, some 2 miles farther west, is some of the grandest and most impressive cliff scenery of Cornwall, especially at **Rosemergy,** whose granite pinnacles and those at Bosigran are the highest in the county.

The main road continues from Zennor through delightful countryside to **Morvah.** The little church has a fourteenth-century tower but the rest of the building dates from George IV's reign. The next village, **Pendeen,** has for long been a centre of the tin-mining industry in West Cornwall. Many famous mines, long closed, such as Levant and Boscaswell have recently been re-opened bringing renewed life to the area.

In a further mile we arrive at Botallack, the site of another great mine. On the headland to the west is **Kenidjack Castle,** an Iron Age stronghold with a well-defined double rampart of stone and earth. The castle headland is the northern horn of **Porthledden Bay;** the southern is **Cape Cornwall,** the only headland designated a cape in England and Wales. Its summit gives a good view of the terrible rocks to the southwest known as **The Brisons,** the scene of many wrecks, and, beyond, of the rugged rocks of the Land's End.

It is 1½ miles from Cape Cornwall to the old mining town of **St Just** which, although somewhat grey in appearance, is the centre of an interesting area and deserves a visit for the sake of its church. It was built in 1336, aisles being added at the end of the fourteenth century. Most of the surviving building dates from the fifteenth century. There are two wall-paintings, much restored, portraying George and the Dragon and Christ blessing the Trades. In the town square, adjoining the War Memorial will be seen a circular enclosure called the **Plane an Gwarry,** the scene in former days of old Cornish miracle plays, wrestling and other sports.

About 2 miles north-east of St Just and the same distance south-east of Pendeen is **Carn Kenidjack,** a famous 'hooting cairn', above a re-markable plain known as the **Gump.**

Beside the road from St Just to Sennen is **Land's End Airport** at Kelynack. Pleasure flights along the coast are operated in summer.

Now the road follows the line of the beautiful **Whitesand Bay.** It is recorded as having been the landing place of both King Stephen and King John. There are some fine cliff walks hereabouts and coast views are delightful. Five miles from St Just and a mile inland from the coast is **Sennen Churchtown.**

Sennen, or 'Churchtown' as it is called, is the most westerly village in England. The place is said to have been the scene of the great encounter with the Danes, the battle of Vellan-Druchet, when King Arthur and the seven Cornish kings or chieftains joined forces. Legend declares that the fight against the sea king was so fierce that not a Norse-man escaped, and that the mill-wheel from which the battle took its name was worked with the blood that rolled seawards. This was the last time the Northmen invaded Cornwall. To celebrate the event, the kings dined at a large rock called the *Table Mén*, situated at the approach to Mayon Farm, on the east side of the main road north of the church.

Parts of the present St Sennen Church date from the thirteenth cen-tury. An inscription on the font refers to the dedication of an addition made in 1430.

Beyond the village and down a very steep incline on the left is the hamlet of **Sennen Cove,** from which there is a bracing cliff-walk to Land's End. It is not really a cove, but a village scattered along the south-ern end of the fine cliff-bound Whitesand Bay. It comprises a few cot-tages, modern houses, stores, cafés and hotels (*Tregiffian*). Some art-ists' studios are evidence of the picturesque appeal of the neighbouring shore, moors and porths. The older part of the village clusters round the quaint capstan house now used as a store for fishermen's gear. Here is a stone pier, which affords a good view of the bay, and the Lifeboat House. There are several car parks. Not least among the pleasures here are the vast sandy beach and beautifully clear water with excellent bath-ing and surfing. The neighbouring moors have great attractions.

Land's End

Car Parking There is a large car park beside the hotels. There is a smaller car park on the right of the approach road. **Hotels** *Hallan Vean, Land's End.*

Rocks at Land's End

It may be that sentiment has a good deal to do with the interest which Land's End excites, for there are many parts of the coast of Cornwall grander and more beautiful; but visitors as a rule feel a certain pleasure in visiting 'the last inn in England' and the neighbouring church at Sennen, and, still farther west, in patronizing absolutely the last house in Britain, and in sitting on the westernmost rocks. The best time for exploring the peninsula is at low tide, as then it is possible, *under the charge of a guide*, to visit the large cavern called the **Land's End Hole.** It is about 150 feet in length, and runs through the promontory, but the channel is so narrow that only in the calmest weather can a boat pass into the cavern. The Land's End coast is far from calm, and it is worth visiting specially during south-west winds.

Within sight of Land's End on a clear day are the Isles of Scilly, twenty-eight miles distant; while nearer, less than two miles west from Land's End, the **Longships Lighthouse** rises from its rocky base, amid the cauldron of waves, to a height of 52 feet above a rock, itself 60 feet high. Seven-and-a-half miles to the south is the **Wolf Rock.**

Both lights are visible for 16 miles. The fog siren on the Long-ships gives a blast of 1½ seconds in every 15 seconds, while the Wolf makes its presence known by a blast of 2½ seconds in every half-minute. Around Land's End are strewn a number of grotesquely-shaped rocks and small islands.

The shortest route from Land's End to Penzance is by the A30, a distance of 10 miles. But by bearing right in ¾ mile from Land's End and joining the B3315 one may travel nearer the coast, passing through Treen.

Walkers are recommended the beautiful cliff walk eastward from Land's End to the Logan Rock.

The first point in this walk is **Carn Creis.** Just off it is the *Dallah* or Dollar Rock, and the rock island a little beyond is the **Armed Knight,** which in certain lights bears some resemblance to a mail-clad giant leaning against the pile, of which a projection forms the bent knees. The other large rock close by is called **Gwelas,** the 'sea-bird's rock.' Due east of these is a point called **Carn Greeb,** the 'comb' or 'crest', from the rough likeness of its crowning ridge of rocks to a cock's comb. Greeb also is the name of the little homestead here. In the field just beyond the cottage flint flakes abound.

The island immediately in front of us and near the cliffs is **Enys Dodman.** Its outer side is pierced by an archway some 40 feet in height. The rock may be reached at low tide by those equal to an awkward bit of cragwork, and then through the arch there may be obtained a fine view of the Armed Knight. In spring the rock is the nesting-place of countless gulls.

Continuing we next reach **Pordenack Point,** a magnificent headland nearly 200 feet above the blue waters to which the cliff falls like a wall. It has the further characteristic of being formed of huge blocks of granite piled one upon the other with amazing regularity, so that gigantic columns are built up.

Beyond Pordenack Point we pass **Carn Voel** and **Carn Evall** with **Zawn Rudh,** the 'red cavern' below, so named from the colour of the rock. Then we have before us the picturesque cove of Nanjizal to which a small brook bounds from rock to rock.

We skirt the bay, and on its southern side, where the cliff edge is quite low, we cross by stepping-stones the stream previously seen. A steep path takes us to the top of Carn lês Boel, the 'carn of the bleak place'. To the south-west of it is the rock island of Bosistow. Next we arrive at **Pendower Cove,** where there is a pile of curious flat boulders and the **Bosistow Logan Stone** on the edge of the cliff. To the south of the cove is a long low point with two or three islets at its extremity. It is called Carn Barra, the 'loaf carn', and from it there is a fine view of the coast in both directions. From it we have a grand walk for a mile, passing Carn Mellyn, the 'yellow carn', Pellitrass Point, Pellow Zawn, Porth Loe Cove, and Carn Guthensbras, the 'great carn', on the farther side of it. Then we arrive at the headland with the formidable name of **Tol-Pedn-Penwith** ('the holed headland in Penwith'), forming the extreme western boundary of Mount's Bay. It vies with Pordenack in boldness, but to be seen when most imposing it must be visited when huge rollers are dashing against its rugged sides. Then the sight is terribly grand. It gains its distinctive name from a great funnel-shaped chasm in a grass-covered neck that joins another mass of rock to the mainland, a few yards to the south-west of the head. The 'Funnel', like the 'Lion's Den' at the Lizard, appears to have been formed by part of the roof of a sea cave falling and the débris being in time washed away. The chasm extends from nearly the top of the high cliff to the sea. It is fairly easy at low water to get down to the mouth of the cave connected with the funnel, but the return is difficult through the presence of a slab 7 feet high on which there is little foothold and this visit should be attempted only by experienced climbers.

The cliffs can be best seen from below, and as they are inclined, not sheer, the descent should be made. The best spot for this is the northern slope at the end of the head. The cliffs on either hand are more magnificent, especially at the **Chair Ladder** of the headland, where cubes upon cubes of granite rise sheer as though built by the Titans.

Continuing our walk we notice on the higher ground, on our left, two iron cores, one red, the other black and white. They are beacons which, when in line, give the direction of a submerged rock known as the Runnel Stone, on which many good ships have met their fate. It is about a mile off the point. On it is a buoy, producing a dismal sound like the mooing of a cow.

Eastward of Tol-Pedn-Penwith is a conical headland, called Polostoc Zawn. It owes its name to the fancied resemblance of one of its rocks to a fisherman's cap. Beyond it we reach the fishing cove of **Porthgwarra,** 'the higher port', famed for lobsters and for two curious tunnels through the cliff on the east connecting the hamlet with the sands. The little settlement is said to be the descendant of a Breton fishing village. The cove is paved with large stones and has remained unspoilt.

From Porthgwarra the cliff path continues in half a mile to **Porth**

St Levan Church, from the south-east

Chapel, so named from a baptistery of St Levan, the scanty ruins of which stand at the head of an ancient stairway down to Porth Chapel beach. An oratory stands nearby on the cliff just before crossing the brook that comes down from **St Levan Churchtown,** ¼ mile up the valley. It is a hamlet, rather than a town, for the place consists merely of the church, the rectory and a farm; though the little cove is beloved by those who have had the fortune to discover it.

The path continues to **Porthcurno Bay,** considered by many to be the most beautiful cove in Cornwall. A green flowery valley leads to a scene of dazzling loveliness—silver sands backed by magnificent cliffs face a beautiful bay where the sea varies in colour from deep purple to jade green and Mediterranean blue.

West of the beach the **Minack Theatre** attracts large numbers of visitors. This open-air Greek-style cliff theatre was inaugurated in 1932. The auditorium is a natural amphitheatre of sloping cliff into which ridges have been cut to form rows of stone and grass seats. The stage has a smooth paved floor, pillars in the Grecian style and an ever-changing backcloth of sea and sky. Greek, Shakespearian and modern plays are performed from March to October.

About ¾ of a mile to the east is **Treen Castle,** a once fortified headland (National Trust). The ancient fort (Treryn Dinas) is approached across the ridge of an isthmus, and still exhibits an earthwork, a triple vallum, and a fosse, forming a triple line of defence. The castle consists of a huge pile of rocks, grotesquely shaped and rising to a great height. On the western side, near the top, is the Logan Rock.

The **Logan Rock** is said to weigh over 65 tons. To reach it a little climbing is necessary, but to those not troubled with over-sensitive nerves there is neither difficulty nor danger, and some who arrive at it may say there is no reward. Dr Borlase, the great Cornish antiquary of the eighteenth century, said of the rock: 'It is morally impossible that any lever, or indeed force however applied in a mechanical way, can remove it from its present situation.' This statement was in 1824 the indirect cause of the stone being overthrown. Lieutenant Goldsmith, a nephew of the poet, when cruising off the coast, determined to prove that Dr Borlase was wrong. Landing with a dozen sailors, he succeeded in dislodging the giant rock, which rumbled down from its lofty perch. This foolhardy action occasioned such indignation in the neighbourhood that the Admiralty compelled the officer to replace the stone. This was done after much exertion and at great expense, but the stone has never 'logged' with the same ease as before. Another stone is called the **Logging Lady.**

The hamlet of **Treen** ½ mile to the north lies just off the B3315 which may be followed to Penzance, keeping left in ¼ mile along the B3283. **St Buryan** is notable for its church, one of the most interesting in West Cornwall. The tower is of four stages and soars 92 feet high. Most of the church dates from the fifteenth century. In the north wall of the sanctuary is a rude arch which is part of the church built in 1238. The south aisle retains much of the ancient carved timbers and wall-plates. In the north aisle is a thirteenth-century tomb with a Norman–French inscription. The most interesting feature of the church is the rood screen which incorporates much of the fine original work. In the upper portion are hunting scenes, warfare between animals and birds and grinning heads. The unusual size of the rood-loft stairway indicates that the rood-loft was used for ceremonial purposes and special choral effects.

In a further 2 miles the road joins the A30 which leads to—

Penzance

Bathing Though the upper parts of the beaches are shingly the bathing is absolutely safe. At low tide large expanses of sand are revealed and here and there are pools among the rocks for the delight of children. The most popular bathing-places are Lariggan Beach and the Western Beach, but good swimmers often prefer to bathe from the Battery Rocks, on account of the diving (but caution is necessary when the tide is less than half). There is also bathing from the sandy beach at the eastern end of the town, known as the Eastern Green, which stretches for three miles around Mount's Bay to Marazion.

Adjoining the Battery Rocks and the 1914–18 War Memorial is a very fine *Open-air Bathing Pool* with diving-boards and other facilities.

There is splendid bathing at most of the little coves on the coast, but local advice should be sought with regard to currents and depth of water. Caution should especially be exercised in rough weather and publicly exhibited danger warnings should be strictly observed.

Bowls Alexandra Grounds and Bolitho Gardens.

Buses There are bus services between Penzance, St Just and Pendeen; Penzance and Land's End; Penzance, St Buryan and Treen; Gurnard's Head and Zennor; Penzance, Lelant and St Ives; Penzance, Porthleven and Helston.

Cinema *Savoy*, Causewayhead.

Distances Bodmin, 46 miles; Camborne, 13; Falmouth, 23; Helston, 13; Land's End, 10; Lizard, 20; London, 280; Newquay, 33; St Ives, 9; Truro, 26.

Early Closing Wednesday.

Golf The nearest links are those of the *West Cornwall Golf Club* at Lelant.

Heliport Isles of Scilly service from Eastern Green heliport.

Hotels *Chypons*, Newlyn; *Minalto; Mount Prospect; Pentrea; Queen's; Union; Yacht Inn.*

Library Morrab Road.

Museums *Geological Museum*, St John's Hall; *Natural History and Antiquarian Museum*, Penlee House; *Nautical Art, and Man O'War Display*, Chapel Street.

Population 19,360.

Tennis Alexandra Grounds, Bolitho Gardens, Penlee Memorial Park.

Tourist Information Centre Alverton Street.

Penzance (*pen-sans*, the holy head) is the metropolis of the toe of England, its chief business and pleasure centre—a town that has prospered amazingly, considering its isolation, for hundreds of years. Up to the middle of the eighteenth century the turnpike road into Cornwall ended at Falmouth, and a writer of that period states that 'there was only one cart in the town of Penzance, and if a carriage occasionally appeared in the streets it attracted universal attention'.

The town is built on the side of a hill on the north-west shore of lovely Mount's Bay, 10 miles from Land's End on the one side and 16 from the Lizard Point direct on the other; and, facing eastwards, it commands the whole expanse of the famous bay, bounded by a succession of undulating hills and sheer cliffs, the continuity broken here and there by coves with sandy beaches. Away toward the horizon may be seen a constant succession of ships making their way to or from the Atlantic. Nearer at hand may probably be seen fishing boats from the neighbouring villages of Newlyn and Mousehole, with perhaps some Plymouth, St Ives, Brixham or East Coast craft.

England has many bays indenting its coast-line, but Mount's Bay stands alone for expansiveness, variety of scene, and last, but by no means least in interest or picturesqueness, for its St Michael's Mount.

In addition to its bay, Penzance possesses a countryside teeming with interest; on each side of it is a coast-line which for grandeur has few equals and it has a climate unsurpassed in the British Isles for its mildness in winter and for its equability at all seasons.

Yet until comparatively recent years Penzance existed mainly as the centre of a rich agricultural district and a wealthy mineral area. It was and is a market town and until 1838 it was the coinage town of the Stannary of Penwith.

The Landing of the Spaniards

Penzance prospered in the sixteenth century, but its fortunes received a check in 1595, when it was pillaged by the Spaniards after they had burned Mousehole and Newlyn. Having escaped the heavy hand of the Spanish Armada, the three little villages were content to think all danger past, when a squadron of Spanish galleys appeared off Mousehole, and two hundred soldiers landed at Mousehole and moved up the hill to Paul. Unprepared for attack, the fishermen fled before the well-trained soldiers, who set the little town on fire and burnt the church of St Paul on the hill. Newlyn suffered a similar fate and then the invading force moved to Penzance. Here, however, resolute resistance was organized by Sir Francis Godolphin and the Spanish forces were compelled to withdraw. The invasion provided the incentive to augment the English militia and to attack and burn Cadiz.

In 1614 James I granted Penzance a charter of incorporation, which is still preserved in the municipal archives. Possessing a market, an annual fair, and a quay, the new borough prospered greatly, and soon out-distanced its rivals—Mousehole, Newlyn and Marazion. Thenceforward Penzance was the metropolis of the peninsula, though Marazion was the older borough, having been incorporated in 1595 by Queen Elizabeth.

When all England was ablaze during the Civil War, Penzance was at first little disturbed, though it remained loyal to the King. But the Penzance people paid dearly for their loyalty. The Parliamentary soldiers seized the town, and it became a scene of plunder and ruin, and was completely sacked; a disaster which befell it again in the following year.

77

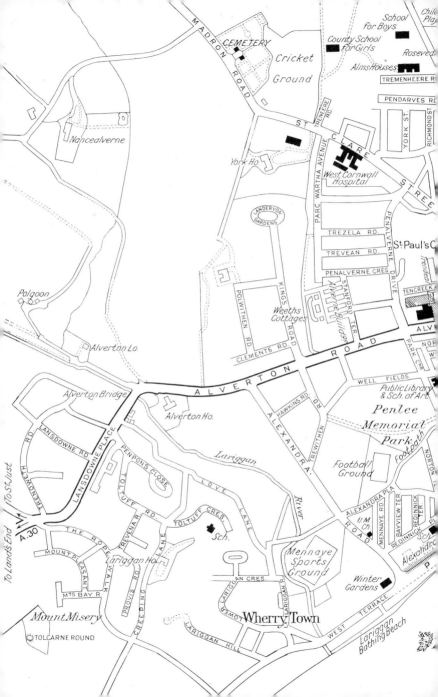

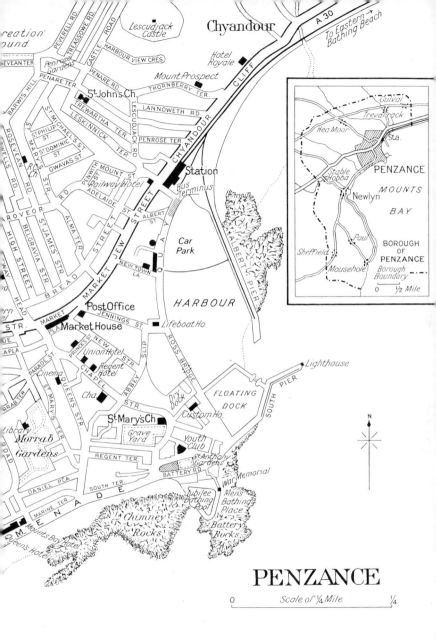

PENZANCE

Scale of ¼ Mile

0   ¼

Inset map labels:

Gulval

Trevaylock

Hea Moor

Sta.

PENZANCE

Stable Hobba

Newlyn

MOUNTS BAY

BOROUGH OF PENZANCE

Sheffield

Paul

Mousehole

Borough Boundary

0   ½ Mile

Main map labels:

Chyandour

A 30

To Eastern Bathing Beach

reation 'ound

EVEAN TER.

PEVERELL RD.

TREASSOWE RD.

CASTLE ROAD

HARBOUR VIEW CRES.

Lescudjack Castle

Hotel Royale

Mount Prospect

Penrose Gardens

PENARE TER.

BARWIS HILL

PENARE RD.

THORNBERRY TER.

St.John's Ch.

TREWARTHA TER.

LANNOWETH RD.

LESKINNICK TER.

St PHILIP ST.

St MICHAEL'S ST.

St DOMINIC ST.

Ro. Ch.

GWAVAS ST.

PENROSE TER.

LESCUDJACK RD.

CLIFF

CHYANDOUR

Station

ROSEVEAN RD.

St MARY'S RD.

PENWITH RD.

MOUNT LA.

Railway Hotel

Railway Station

Bus Terminus

ROVEOR RD.

BELGRAVIA STR.

St JAMES' STR.

ADELAIDE ST.

ALMA TER.

ALBERT ST.

Car Park

HIGH STREET

BREAD STR.

JEW STREET

MARKET STREET

NEWTOWN LA.

ALBERT PIER

HARBOUR

STR.

MARKET PLA.

Post Office

JENNINGS ST.

Lifeboat Ho.

Market House

APLA

PARADE ST.

Cinema

PRINCES STR.

NEW STR.

Union Hotel

SLIP

ROSS BRIDGE

Lighthouse

CHAPEL ST.

Regent Hotel

Cha.

ABBEY STR.

Dry Dock

FLOATING DOCK

SOUTH PIER

RABTER

St MARY'S TER.

QUEENS STR.

St Mary's Ch.

Custom Ho.

Library

Morrab Gardens

Grave Yard

Youth Club

St Anthony Gardens

REGENT TER.

War Memorial

DANIEL PLA.

SOUTH TER.

BATTERY RD.

Men's Bathing Place

MARINE TER.

Jubilee Bathing Pool

Battery Rocks

ROAD

PROMENADE

Mounts Bay Hotel

Chimney Rocks

Queen's Hotel

N

When the persecutions of the Penzance people which marked the years of the Commonwealth were at an end, Charles II, as a recompense for its loyalty, made it a coinage town—that is, a town to which all tin within the Stannary of Penwith and Kerrier had to be brought to have a coin, or corner, cut off, that its quality might be tested. Up to 1838, every hundredweight of metal was thus dealt with and taxed four shillings. In this way the Duchy of Cornwall received about £10,000 a year.

During the seventeenth century, and even as late as the middle of the following century, Penzance was subject to visits of piratical bands—Turkish, Algerian and French.

For the last two centuries Penzance has been left in peace to develop into a pleasant, clean, friendly place—a town of lovely gardens and clusters of small grey stone houses nestling in the curve of beautiful Mount's Bay.

The Town

The A30 Land's End road runs through the town and part of it is **Market Jew Street** where are the town's main shops, post office and the Market House, a domed granite building part occupied by a bank. In front of its classical façade stands a **statue of Sir Humphry Davy,** the world-famous inventor of the miner's safety lamp, who was born at Penzance in a house almost opposite where the monument now stands. A plaque has been placed on the wall of the property, now a shop, though some authorities contend that his birthplace was Varfell near Ludgvan.

Nearby is the **Guildhall** with the **Museum** (*June to September, week-day mornings*) of the Royal Geological Society of Cornwall, the second oldest geological society in the world, established in 1814. Numerous minerals are on display and collections of rock specimens and fossils. The block also contains St John's Hall, used for various functions.

The **Museum of Nautical Art** (*April to October, daily 10–1, 2–4; charge*) houses treasure recovered from a squadron of ships that sank in 1707. There is also a **Man O' War Display** showing a section in life size of a four-deck warship of 1730.

On the seaward side of Alverton Street, midway between the Market House and the Municipal Buildings, is a road leading to the northern entrance of the **Morrab Gardens,** of which the lower end is only two minutes from the sea front. This retreat is not merely a well-kept little park but a standing advertisement of the climate of the town. Probably no public grounds in England can equal the display, in the open air, of so many sub-tropical plants. There is a fine show of palms, and the aloe, myrtle, geranium, camellia and many other plants thrive out of doors all the year round. A band plays here on Sundays during the summer months and concerts by choirs and visiting bands are also held.

In the nearby mansion is the **Penzance Library** to which members subscribe. It has a vast collection and is well stocked with books on Cornwall and Devon.

Near the upper end of Morrab Road, west of the Gardens, are the **School of Art,** and the **Public Library.** In front of the Library is an ancient bronze cannon found at Low Lee in 1916. It was part of the armament of a ship of the Spanish Armada. Upon it is a rosary by means of which it has been possible to identify the ship which carried the gun.

To the west of the Morrab Gardens is the **Penlee Memorial Park.** This fifteen-acre parkland forms the town's War Memorial. Five acres have been set aside for games and recreation and there are several hard and grass tennis courts on which open tournaments are played. There are children's playgrounds, a walled Garden of Remembrance, shady walks, well-placed seats and an attractive *Open-air Theatre.* Adjoining the Park is a football ground—reputed to be the finest in Cornwall.

Just inside the entrance to the park is **Penlee House Museum** (*week-days 12.30–4.30*) in which are exhibited natural history specimens from the neighbourhood and relics of the town's history.

The Sea Front

From the Park, Morrab Road and Alexandra Road lead to the Promenade. At the lower end of Alexandra Road is the **Penzance Club** and hard by, the starting point of many of the coaches and buses. The sea-front commands an extensive and magnificent view. On one side the sea-scape is bordered by the steep-sloping hills of Penlee Point, on the other it stretches away to the Lizard, and the broad expanse of Mount's Bay is dominated by the castellated height of St Michael's Mount.

From Alexandra Road, the sea-front curves south-west to Newlyn. Between the road and the beach are the **Bolitho Gardens,** luxuriant with palm trees and beautiful plants. Here, too, are hard tennis courts, a bowling green, putting green, shelters and seats. Eastward from Alexandra Road are the **Alexandra Grounds** with a fine bowling rink, putting green and tennis courts. Adjoining is the **Grand Casino.** A large café-restaurant with a fine view of the Promenade occupies the ground floor. Farther east, the Promenade becomes Battery Road. Here are the terraced **St Anthony Gardens** with lovely flower beds and a massive granite fountain weighing 23 tons. The gardens occupy the site of the ancient chapel of St Anthony. The elevated terrace in these gardens is called Coinagehall Walk in commemoration of the old Coinage Hall which stood nearby from the time of Charles II for about two hundred years. Opposite is the **Jubilee Bathing Pool.** There are sun-bathing terraces, a café, a separate corner for children and high-diving platforms. Galas and water polo matches are held weekly in the season.

Nearby are the **Battery Rocks,** named after a minor fortification built in 1740. Here is a popular open-air bathing-place. On a narrow pier-like projection the coastguards used to practise gunnery, and on the site of their battery has been erected the local 1914–1918 **War Memorial,** a column of granite blocks on a granite pedestal bearing the names of those who fell.

The **Harbour** is tidal and though not large is a busy and interesting place and its quays are favourite promenades. Of interest are the buoys which are brought in for maintenance by the Trinity House depot. Boat excursions to the bay and St Michael's Mount start from here.

Overlooking the harbour is **St Mary's Church** in a fine situation and dating from 1834.

Excursions from Penzance

I. To Newlyn, Mousehole and Lamorna
Newlyn, which lies a mile west along the shore is, together with Mousehole, 2 miles farther, incorporated in the borough of Penzance. For long a quiet village with great attraction for artists it has now grown to be a busy fishing town.

The harbour, however, still presents a colourful picture. Here come sails of all hues, craft of all shapes and designs and sailors from many lands. Along the quayside, nets are mended, boats and buoys painted, fish unloaded and packed in boxes. From the quay twist up the steep and narrow cobbled streets with here and there a quaint old building worthy of note. The tiny original quay (now enclosed in a fine extensive harbour) and the magnificent views over Penzance and round Mount's Bay add to the interest.

The boundary between Penzance and Newlyn is marked by the **Newlyn Art Gallery** (*weekdays 10–1, 2–5; free*). The gallery stands beside the main coastal road and was specifically built for the artists of Newlyn. As well as a permanent collection of paintings, pottery and sculpture, there are frequent exhibitions of contemporary works by leading West Country artists.

Beyond the gallery are cross-roads and to the left is the picturesque **Ship Institute.** Beyond it are the quay, the fish landing stage and the fish market. Clustering round the water-side are cottages, warehouses and other buildings with a maze of quaint courts, alleys, archways and gardens.

From Newlyn the coastal road passes the Penlee Quarries and continues to Mousehole, 2 miles from Newlyn. On the left is passed **Penlee Point** where there is a lifeboat station open for inspection. South of the point is **St Clement's Isle** forming a natural, useful breakwater at the mouth of Mousehole Harbour. It is reputed to have been the abode of a hermit from whom the island gets its name.

Mousehole (*Cairn D'hu, Lobster Pot, Old Coastguard*)—pronounced *mow-sell*—was once a trading port of importance, but is now a quaint village with twisting little streets. The small harbour used to be busy with fishing boats but the industry has dwindled almost to nothing and the craft are mainly for pleasure purposes. The oldest building in Mousehole is known as the **Keigwin Arms,** now a private residence. It was formerly a manor house, then a licensed hostelry. In spite of considerable restorations in 1946–7 it is still an excellent example of Elizabethan style domestic architecture. As far back as 1595, when the Spaniards surprised the good people of the village and burnt the church of Paul on the hill, this house was in existence, and in it reposed the cannonball which is said to have killed the owner, Jenkin Keigwin by name. A sword owned by him is exhibited in the Penzance Museum. The walls of the Keigwin Arms are of the old-fashioned solid order, four feet thick, and tradition states that the timbers grew in the forest, now submerged, that surrounded St Michael's Mount. To reach the house follow the road round the harbour passing the War Memorial on the left. Continue straight for 200 yards to a T-junction. The house stands almost directly opposite.

On the coast, about ten minutes' walk from the Keigwin Arms, is **Mousehole Cave.** Although somewhat difficult of access, it receives a few visitors.

About 1 mile north-west of Mousehole is the village of **Paul.** Against the gate opposite the south-east corner of the church is a granite obelisk commemorating the life and death of Dorothy Pentreath, commonly said to have been the last person to have spoken the old Cornish language, though there are rival claimants in William Bodener of Mousehole and John Davey (1812–91) of Boswednack near Zennor. The church contains one scarred arch of an earlier building burnt by the Spaniards in 1595. In the south aisle is a Cornish epitaph to Captain Stephen Hutchens, who left a bequest for the Church and for the erection of an Almshouse called the *Gift House* adjoining the church. The stone is dated 1709. The inscription is probably the only one extant in the county, of all those which were set up while the Cornish language was in use. It runs thus:

Bounas heb dueth, Eu poes karens wei
Tha Pobl Bohodzhak Paull Han Egles nei.

The epitaph has been translated:

'Eternal life be his whose loving care
Gave Paul an almshouse and the Church repair.'

From Mousehole the road climbs steeply and then bends to the right. At a T-junction turn left for **Lamorna.** The flowery valley of Lamorna with its trout stream, cascades and picturesque rocky cove is popular with artists. Many of them have made their home at Lamorna and an exhibition of local artists is usually held during the summer. There are natural pools for bathing and a sandy beach is exposed at low tide.

This is an interesting area for prehistoric monuments. To see two of them take the road north from the valley and turn left at the main road. As a hill is climbed the Pipers, two pillar stones about 12 feet high and 120 feet apart, peer over a wall on the right just beyond the farm as the road bends to the right. They were the men who made the music for the dancing maidens—the **Merry Maidens**—who now appear in the guise of a circle of nineteen stones, and all because they made merry on a Sunday. This Bronze Age stone circle can be seen in a field on the left about $\frac{1}{2}$ mile beyond the Pipers.

The stones are near to the hamlet of **Boleigh** (belay). The name signifies 'a place of slaughter' and the spot to which it has been given is said to be that where Athelstan finally vanquished the Cornish in 936. At Boleigh is a remarkable *fougou* (underground passage, or cave) lined and roofed with slabs of granite. (Private land; permission necessary.)

The return to Penzance may be made by the B3315.

Lamorna is a good starting point for a coastal walk to the Logan Rock ($5\frac{1}{2}$ miles). The first point reached after leaving Lamorna along the coast is **Tater-du.** Thence we go round a bay and across a combe to **Boscawen Point,** where granite is finely piled up, and the end of our trip is in view, for **Treryn** (*treen*) **Dinas,** the site of the Logan Rock, stands boldly out to sea a couple of miles to the westward. From Boscawen Point we turn away a little from the cliffs to avoid bad going and then descend into a charming little wooded valley by which we rejoin the coast at **St Loy's Cove.** Sheltered from the north and west winds by tree-clad hills and from the east winds by Boscawen Point, and faced by the warm sea-water, it is, in winter, one of the warmest spots in England.

From the top of the next headland, **Merthen Point,** we look right into **Penberth Cove,** a wild and picturesque spot, with its giant boulders on every hand and its 'beach' paved with great flat stones to form a slipway for the small motor-boats used by the local fishermen. A large windlass at the head of the slipway; a few very substantially built stone cottages; some lobster pots, fishing nets and other gear complete an attractive scene. But the Cove is a mile away, and between us and it are a pair of combes and the headland of *Pedn sa wanack*. On the western side of Penberth cove is **Cribba Head,** 'the crested head', and ½ a mile farther is **Treryn Dinas** and the Logan Rock (see page 75).

II. To Sancreed

From **Drift,** 2½ miles along the main road westward from Penzance, a road on the right leads to Sancreed. On the right of this road is a fine dam and reservoir (1961) supplying the water needs of the Land's End peninsula.

Sancreed village consists of little more than the fine fifteenth-century church embowered in trees in a lovely setting. The chancel has a beautiful panelled and carved roof. The rood screen includes old panels with quaint carvings, showing a goat among thistles, a jester blowing a trumpet and other amusing subjects. In the churchyard is a beautifully ornamented eleventh-century cross, and on the churchyard wall is a Celtic-style wheel cross.

Between Sancreed and the A30 is a fine menhir known as the **Blind Fiddler.** About ½ mile to the south and across the main road is an important Bronze Age stone circle—**Boscawen-Un.** Here the Cornish bards meet for the colourful ceremony of the Gorsedd which is conducted in the Cornish language.

About 1 mile to the west of Sancreed is **Carn Euny,** the site of an Iron Age settlement. Nearby, at **Brane,** is a good example of a chambered round barrow.

III. To Madron and Lanyon Quoit

Leave Penzance by the B3312 Madron road which leads in 1 mile to **Heamoor,** a village in which John Wesley preached, standing on a rock which is the pulpit of the chapel erected by his followers. About ½ mile to the west lies **Trengwainton Garden** (*March to September, Wednesday, Thursday, Friday, Saturday and Bank Holiday Mondays 11–6; charge*). Originally laid out in the first half of the nineteenth century but transformed after 1925, these grounds, owned by the National Trust, include a fine collection of rhododendrons and many delicate shrubs from all over the world.

As we ascend towards Madron there is a foretaste of the fine views over Mount's Bay which are a feature of this excursion.

Madron Church, 2½ miles from Penzance Promenade and 380 feet above sea-level, is the mother church of Penzance, the village being a much older place than the now flourishing town. The building replaced one of Norman architecture which was held by the Knights Hospitallers of St John. The oldest parts are the font and the Norman base of a pillar at the east end of the south aisle. The rood-stair doorway is in the south aisle, and on the opposite side of the church is a corresponding recess. Most of the woodwork (linen-fold bench-ends in the body of the church, side screens of chancel and low chancel screen) is modern, but a few pieces of old carving are worked into the chancel screen, and in the south aisle of the chancel are fourteenth-century bench-ends, found under the floor.

To reach **Madron Well and Baptistery,** go through the village and then take a right turn in about ½ mile. This becomes a track with signposts to both sites. Little remains of the fourteenth-century Baptistery, reduced to ruins by the Puritans, except the walls and, inside, fragments of stone seats and the altar slab. The **Wishing Well** was traditionally visited by village maidens on May Morning.

Lanyon Quoit is one of the finest megalithic monuments in England in spite of the damage that has been done to it. It stands to the right of the Morvah road about 2 miles beyond Madron looking, in the distance, like a bench. The cromlech consists of a capstone 17 feet 4 inches long, 8 feet 9 inches wide and 1 foot 6 inches thick, supported on three granite slabs about 5 feet high. Originally a horseman could ride beneath it, but in 1815 it was overthrown by a violent storm. In 1824 it was replaced by the machinery used in replacing the Logan Rock, but not at its original height, thus destroying much of the archaeological interest of the monument. It is now owned by the National Trust.

From Lanyon a track goes north-eastward to the **Ding Dong Mine,** the oldest and most romantic deserted mine in the county. The disused engine-house is a sufficient guide. The hill on which it stands affords a magnificent view.

On the hill north of the mine, about ½ mile from it (go first north-east and then north), are the remains of a stone circle called the **Nine Maidens,** 6 miles from Penzance. Only six of the original twenty-two stones are erect. The south side of the circle is interrupted by a low cairn, near the centre of which are the remains of a small cist.

For **Mulfra Quoit** we go eastward from the Nine Maidens to Mulfra Hill. The two points are about a mile apart. On the south-east side of the hill is the quoit or cromlech. The capstone has fallen, but three sides of the cist it covered remain. From it the return can be made to Penzance (4 miles) by the Zennor road.

IV. To Gulval, Castle-an-Dinas and Chysauster

Leave Penzance by the A30 Marazion road which leads in about ½ mile to Chyandour. The simplest route then is to continue along the main road for another ¼ mile and then turn to the left. Gulval will be reached in less than ¼ mile. A more attractive route for pedestrians is by the path leaving the Marazion road at Branwell Lane about 130 yards beyond Chyandour. Some of the best agricultural land in England is in **Gulval** and the flower industry is very important. The church is one of the most beautifully situated in the country. The churchyard, largely shaded by trees, is brightened by many sub-tropical plants—dracænas, yuccas, hydrangeas, and others—while flourishing palms bear testimony to the mildness of the climate. It is an old church, carefully restored and greatly embellished by the Bolitho family, the many memorials to whom, all worked in warm-veined Derbyshire felspar, give a distinct richness to the interior. The north lych-gate is composed of the arcading of the twelfth-century transept.

The lane opposite the north side of Gulval Church climbs steeply and in about a mile reaches *Badger's Cross*, where we take the right-hand road, and follow it for ½ mile to the hamlet of Castle Gate. Here a road on the right comes up from Ludgvan, and opposite a track goes between houses on the left and, after rounding the south side of a huge quarry, up to Castle-an-Dinas; or follow the road for another ½ mile and take the track to the left just after the road has made a sharp left-hand turn and before it goes to the right again. **Castle-an-Dinas** (765 feet) is interesting as the site of a hill-fort, but its more general appeal

87

is based upon the really magnificent views over Mount's Bay and a great part of west Cornwall.

The remnants of walls of the fort enclose the foundations of circular huts and a well. The modern square tower serves as a direction-point for those tramping over the moor. It was built in the eighteenth century by the owner of the land.

It is a pleasant walk of about a mile from the top of Castle-an-Dinas, following round the south-side of the huge dump of quarry-waste, to Chysauster, towards the south-west. The road route to Chysauster branches off at Badger's Cross. About ½ a mile beyond the point where wires cross the lane, a notice board on the right indicates the path leading in a few hundred yards to the remains of **Chysauster,** an ancient village that is now the property of the nation. (*March and October, weekdays 9.30–5.30, Sunday 2–5.30; April, daily 9.30–5.30; May to September, daily 9.30–7; November to February, weekdays 9.30–4, Sunday 2–4; charge*).

This prehistoric village was inhabited in the two centuries between 100 B.C. and A.D. 100; it has been partially excavated on more than one occasion. Two of the houses have long been known to visitors, a third was excavated in 1928 and since then five more have been uncovered. The eight houses range either side of a wide street and are imposing stone-built structures, 70 to 90 feet in length and with walls still 3 to 6 feet in height, and in places, 15 feet thick. The principal feature is a large open court into which open small stone-roofed, side chambers; at the end of the court is the principal living-room, containing the household quern-stone, which was probably covered by a wooden roof. In one house the quern has been built up into the jamb of the entrance to the living-room, but its usual position was in the centre of the chamber's floor. The excavation of 1928 revealed obvious traces of a busy tin-washing industry on the site, and no doubt in 'towns' such as this the earliest Cornish tin-workers made their home. Associated with the 'town' are the remains of a *fougou*, or subterranean stone-lined passage, apparently once connecting the village with the tin-stream in the valley.

From Chysauster, Penzance, 4 miles distant, may be regained by the Zennor road by way of New Mill and **Trevaylor,** a total distance of over 9 miles. On regaining the road from the Hut cluster turn to the right; turn left at the corner by Carnquidden Farm and left again on reaching the St Ives road by a quarry to New Mill. From Trevaylor a glorious view of Mount's Bay is obtained and it is itself a lovely valley.

Penzance to Falmouth

The Penzance to Falmouth road is the A394 running through Marazion and Helston.

Marazion is a pleasant place for those who prefer more simplicity than even a genial town like Penzance can give, while still having good facilities for boating, bathing and fishing. And some of its visitors may be drawn to it by its reputation of being one of the warmest places in the country.

St Michael's Mount

Approaches Bus services between Penzance and Marazion. During the summer motor-boats ply from Penzance Quay to St Michael's Mount. Boats may be hired from Marazion beach for the trip to the Mount when the tide is in and the causeway is covered, which is usually for some 16 hours out of the 24. A ferry service operates in summer.
Admission November to March, Monday, Wednesday and Friday by guided tours only. Tours leave at 11, 12, 2, 3 and 4 (weather and tide permitting since no ferry service in winter). April to October, Monday, Wednesday and Friday by free flow, 10.30–5.45 (last admission 4.45); Tuesday by guided tours only. Tours leave at frequent intervals 10.30–4.45. Charge.

St Michael's Mount is a lofty isolated mass of rock, some 21 acres in extent, excluding the foreshore, separated from Marazion at high water by about 500 yards of sea, but at low water connected with the mainland by a stone causeway. Its solitariness and grandeur suggest something of the romantic story that has been woven round it during hundreds of years. The property is now in the ownership of the National Trust.

At its base the Mount is slightly more than a mile in circumference. It rises to a height of over 230 feet above sea-level, where it is crowned by the picturesque castellated mansion of the St Aubyns, with its conspicuous square tower and pretty chapel. Along the northern base are several houses and cottages inhabited principally by fishermen and the retainers of Lord St Levan, with the harbour and two piers on the north side.

Boats loading up to take holidaymakers to St Michael's Mount, from Marazion, near Penzance

The harbour was formerly busy with tin and copper transport and later with china clay. Now there is little business done. The local population numbers about fifty.

At one time the only way up to the castle was by the rough cobbled path up which the public go, but for many years now a light railway has been used to bring stores landed at the harbour through a tunnel under the Mount. On the way is passed a well which supplied the castle with water. There are batteries of guns near the summit. There are also to be seen brass guns taken from a French vessel in 1795. They are fired on special occasions of celebration.

The **Castle** occupies the site of the ancient Benedictine Priory (twelfth to fifteenth century). It has been greatly modernized for family residence. The principal feature is the Chevy Chase Hall, at one time the refectory of the monks.

The **Chapel,** in the Transition style, has been greatly improved and beautified in late years. It has some interesting old glass but that in the windows in the chancel and in the fifteenth-century rose window is fairly modern and commemorates members of the present family.

On the other side of the chapel is a door at the foot of the narrow spiral flight of steps that leads up to the top of the tower, from which a splendid view may be obtained. At the top of this tower is what is called **St Michael's Chair.** It is the ruin of a stone lantern from which a beacon-light used long ago to be exhibited for the benefit of the fishermen. The real 'chair' is on a crag on the west side of the Mount.

The door opening on to the Chapel terrace is guarded by a portcullis.

The History of the Mount. Leland carries the history of the Mount back to a very early date, when St Michael the Archangel is supposed to have appeared there to a hermit. Coins of Roman times have been discovered—pointing to the fact that the Mount was known to those early visitors to Britain. To this romantic spot St Keyne is said to have come on a pilgrimage from Ireland in 490, the spot having been hallowed by the above-mentioned appearance of the Archangel Michael. Edward the Confessor granted it to the Abbey of St Michel on the Normandy coast, to which the Mount bears a striking likeness, and a Priory of Benedictines was established here.

During past centuries St Michael's played its part as a fastness as well as a shrine and sanctuary. In the time of Henry VI, the Earl of Oxford, the Lancastrian leader, fled to this castle after the battle of Barnet, gaining admission in the dress of a pilgrim, and made a stout resistance until, on a promise of pardon, he surrendered the castle. Twenty years later, when Perkin Warbeck landed at Sennen and was hailed by the excited Cornish people as Richard IV, he placed his wife, Lady Catherine Gordon, 'The Fair Rose of Scotland,' as she was called, in St Michael's Mount, while he and his followers marched towards London to claim the throne—with what success history records. Fifty years later, when Cornwall rose against the use of the Reformed Prayer Book, St Michael's Mount was the centre of much fighting. Again in the Civil War it was stoutly attacked by the Parliamentarians, and not less stoutly defended by the Royalists, but eventually the commander, Sir Arthur Basset, an ancestor of a family still honoured in the county, was forced to capitulate and hand over his castle to the Roundheads under Colonel Hammond. With the subsequent fall of Pendennis Castle, Falmouth, after desperate fighting, the Royalist cause in Cornwall collapsed.

In 1659 Colonel John St Aubyn purchased the Mount from Sir Arthur Basset. A descendant, Sir John St Aubyn, was raised to the peerage in 1887 and assumed the title of Baron St Levan. In 1954 Lord St Levan presented the Mount to the National Trust.

A left fork along the B3280 1 mile east of Marazion leads to Goldsithney, site of the **Museum of Mechanical Music** (*Monday to Wednesday 10.30–5.30, 7.30–9.30; Thursday to Saturday 10.30–5.30; Sunday 2–5.30*). Conducted tours and live demonstrations are given of the more than sixty instruments on display, including fairground organs, barrel organs, music boxes and café orchestrions.

Leave Marazion by the A394 and in about 1 mile a road to the right leads to the village of **Perranuthnoe,** picturesquely situated on a hillside above a low cliff. At low tide there is a good stretch of sand popular with bathing and picnic parties. The church has a thirteenth-century granite font.

Return to the main road and after a further mile turn right at Rosudgeon (*Courtlands*) for Prussia Cove. The eastern boundary of Mount's Bay is Cudden Point, on which are **Piskies Cove,** a fine chasm riddled with caves, into which the sea rolls with grand effect in rough weather; **Bessy's Cove,** once the site of an inn frequented by smugglers and kept by one Bessy Burrows; and the more famous **Prussia Cove.** Prussia Cove is a very popular little spot. There is good boating and fishing, and the rocks are convenient for diving and for sun-bathing. Cars have to be parked in a field at the top of the narrow, hilly lane and path leading down to the Cove (free).

Early in 1947 the famous battleship H.M.S. *Warspite*, while being towed round the coast to the ship-breakers, broke away in a terrific gale and went aground during a spring tide on the formidable rocks at this point. In the eighteenth century the Cove was the headquarters of a band of smugglers whose leader, John Carter, was called by his followers the King of Prussia, after the hero of those times. Hence the name of the Cove.

Return to the main road and in a further mile another turning to the right leads to **Praa Sands** (*Prah Sands*). This sandy bay lying eastward to Mount's Bay extends from Hoe Point and Kenneggy Beach to Rinsey Head and Rinsey Cove. The spot offers good bathing but there is some danger due to 'ridging' of the sands and visitors are advised to respect the advice of the local lifeguards regarding tides, currents etc. It is a popular resort, particularly with caravanners. The curious name originated as Pras Sands—Pras meaning a common or meadow. From the sands a lane leads past the restored **Pengersick Castle** (*not open*), associated with many old Cornish stories.

Breage Church. The painting of St Christopher on the north wall

Just off the main road to the right on the way to Helston is **Breage** where the church is well worth a visit. Grotesque heads and gargoyles adorn the tower below the battlements. A Roman milestone with inscription is preserved but the most interesting feature is the startling fifteenth-century wall-paintings. They include depictions of St Christopher, St Hilary, St Corentine and St Ambrose and a Warning to Sabbath-Breakers showing Christ squeezing blood from his heart over tools of various trades.

Helston

Buses To Falmouth, Camborne, Redruth, Penzance and the Lizard.
Early Closing Wednesday.

Hotels *Angel*, *Gwealdues*.
Market Day Monday (cattle market).
Population 10,570.

Helston, by reason of its situation, its antiquity and business accommodation, is one of Cornwall's important market towns. It appears to have existed in the time of King Alfred and was long a walled city, with a castle. The earliest-known charter was granted by King John, to whom the men of Helston gave forty silver marks and a palfrey (1201). In Stuart days, when Killigrew commenced the building of Falmouth, Helston petitioned the King that the work might cease, fearing rivalry to Helston trade. Edward I created 'Helleston' a coinage town for tin, and the Hall stood in Coinage Hall Street until the beginning of the nineteenth century. In 1548 the Cornish insurrection commenced at Helston, headed by Hugh Arundel, Governor of St Michael's Mount, who was defeated at the siege of Exeter and executed. Helston was a very important mining centre until the middle of the nineteenth century.

Helston is a good centre for the tourist, with tennis courts and putting and bowling greens, while grand walks abound in the neighbourhood. It is at its most interesting, however, on May 8th, the **Flora** or **Furry Day** (possibly from the Cornish *feur*, a fair, or holiday).

Formerly the townsfolk and people from the countryside, garlanded with flowers and headed by fiddlers, danced through the streets and in and out of the houses, and this custom has been revived in modified form. For the dancing which follows, music is furnished by the Helston Town Band. Some residents take a holiday for the great occasion. Business is forgotten for a time and traffic is brought to a standstill as the streets become even more tightly packed with the townsfolk—reinforced by sightseers from many miles around. Flora Day at Helston is heralded by the early morning ringing of the parish church bells and the first Furry Dance usually commences at 7 a.m. At ten o'clock the children of the various schools dance through the town, and at twelve o'clock is the dance of the day—the last usually takes place at 5 p.m. The 'Furry dance' air is widely known; once heard, it is not soon forgotten.

St Michael's Church was entirely rebuilt by Earl Godolphin in 1763. An unusual feature is the twenty-four branch chandelier, a gift from the Earl of Godolphin in 1763. The east window, dedicated in 1938, includes two angels dancing the Furry Dance, the opening bars of which also appear in musical notation.

Near the top of the hill (marked by a plaque over the doorway and a letter-box in the wall) is the cottage in which Robert (Bob) Fitzsimmons the famous boxer was born in 1863.

The **Museum** contains an interesting collection of ancient agricultural implements and craft tools, pictures and photographs of local scenes and events etc. The rocket life-saving apparatus of the early pioneer Henry Trengrouse is there and also an enormous cider press.

At Wendron 3 miles north of Helston on the B3297 Redruth road is **Wendron Forge** (*October to May, daily 10–5; June to September, daily 10–9; charge*). There are extensive displays of restored and working antique machines, spacious art and craft showrooms, demonstrations by craftsmen and a restaurant and garden centre.

About 5 miles north-west of Helston between Townshend and Godolphin Cross stands **Godolphin House** (*June and July, Thursday 2–5; August and September, Tuesday and Thursday 2–5; charge*). Parts of the house, once the home of the Earls of Godolphin, date from the early Tudor period and additions were made in Elizabethan and Carolean times. The fine colonnaded front completed shortly before the Civil War rests on massive granite columns.

The B3304 leads from Helston to **Porthleven,** a pretty fishing port at the head of a combe which is well known for its rich growth of semi-tropical flowers. The fishing at Porthleven is first class and there is boating and bathing from the beach of rather coarse sand. On a calm day this is a beautiful corner of Mount's Bay but the sea can be fearsome in winter. In fact the stretch of coast between the Lizard and Land's End has been a trap for ships since navigation began.

To reach Loe Pool a mile or so east of Porthleven, follow the B3304 to the far end of Lower Green where on the left is a stone gate marked

'Private path to Penrose'. This is a beautiful walk and leads through the grounds of Penrose (no dogs or cars) to **Loe Pool.** This, the largest lake in Cornwall, makes a beautiful picture, with the thickly wooded hills mirrored on its surface. It is said to be the lake into which King Arthur's sword Excalibur was thrown, according to Tennyson.

The path continues to the sands at **Loe Bar** with fine views across Mount's Bay.

Leave Helston by the A394 which leads in 10 miles to **Penryn.** Long famous for its granite, it stands at the head of the River Penryn on which Falmouth old town is built. The quays are still generally busy with shipping but there was a time when Penryn was the predominant port in these parts. In the town hall are the old stocks and the museum in the Market Place contains a horse-drawn fire engine and other items of local interest.

In the northern part of the town and near the river is **St Gluvias** church with a fifteenth-century granite tower. Inside is a brass dating from 1489 with the figures of Thomas Kyllygrewe and his wives.

The pretty **College Woods** close to Penryn station are a favourite picnic resort. Ferns grow here in profusion, and during springtime few places in the area are more gorgeously decked with primroses and bluebells. The woods take their name from the scanty remains of Glasney College which was founded in the thirteenth century.

In a further 2 miles we arrive at—

Falmouth

Bathing Gyllyngvase Beach at the western end of Cliff Road. At the Pendennis end of Cliff Road is Castle Beach and there are also popular beaches at Swanpool and Maenporth.
Bowls Recreation Ground, Dracaena. Avenue. Visitors welcomed by Falmouth Bowling Club.
Buses Services to many parts of Cornwall from the bus station in The Moor.
Cinema *ABC*, Market Street.
Distances Helston, 13 miles; Land's End, 36; Lizard via Gweek, 19; London, 267; Newquay, 26; Penzance, 26; Redruth, 11; St Ives, 25; Truro, 11.

Early Closing Wednesday.
Entertainments Band performances in Gyllyngdune Gardens; variety shows, concerts and dancing at the Princess Pavilion. Plays at Falmouth Arts Theatre.
Golf *Falmouth Golf Club*, Pennance Headland.
Hotels *Bay, Carthion, Crill House, Falmouth, Green Bank, Green Lawns, Gwendra, Gyllyngdune, Madeira, Melville, Palm Beach, Pendower, Rosslyn, Royal Duchy, Somerdale, Southcliffe, Suncourt, Tresillian House.*
Information Bureau The Moor.
Library The Moor.

Population 17,530.
Tennis Public courts at rear of Gyllyngvase Beach. Visitors welcome at Falmouth Tennis Club.

Yachting The Royal Cornwall Yacht Club welcomes visitors. There are several other sailing clubs in the area.

Falmouth, the largest town in Cornwall, is beautifully situated on the estuary of the River Fal, with a safe harbourage called **Carrick Roads.** Its equable climate makes it a popular resort in both summer and winter.

Falmouth is not of great antiquity. Sir Walter Raleigh was the first to draw attention to the possibilities of the Fal estuary as a deep-water harbour on a large scale. Developments were hotly opposed by the ports of Truro and Penryn, but these were over-ruled and a settlement started, called Falmouth. In the days of sailing ships, Falmouth became an important Mail Packet Station. Later the importance of the port declined considerably. But in 1863 the construction of the railway brought Falmouth into touch with other parts of the country, and the natural beauty of the place, and its mild climate, led to its growth as a holiday resort.

The hilly nature of the promontory gives the town a great advantage over other seaport resorts by providing two entirely different outlooks— to the north the busy harbour with its quays and dockyards, backed by the tree-fringed Fal; on the south a magnificent prospect of sea and cliffs unsullied by the chimneys and other less beautiful adjuncts of a seaport.

The **Railway Station** is near the junction of **Avenue** and **Melvill Roads;** those who arrive by road will probably enter the town by the shrub-bordered **Dracaena Avenue,** which strikes up to the right soon after passing Penryn. Melvill Road continues Dracaena Avenue and runs along the ridge to the promontory. Any of the pleasant roads to the right lead to the **Cliff Road** bordering Falmouth Bay, where are the bathing beaches and other holiday attractions. The wooded slopes of **Pendennis Point** enclose the bay to the east—the walk or drive round the Head is probably the most interesting of its kind in England. Among the trees below the red-brick barracks are the **Melville Gardens,** an admirable place in which to loiter. The views through the foliage and across the blue bay to the Lizard coast are delightful. From the Gardens one has a good view of Falmouth's sea front and pleasure beaches. Almost at one's feet is the **Castle Beach.**

Gyllyngvase Beach is easily the most popular of the beaches. At the rear is a car park, and adjoining this **Queen Mary Gardens,** with miniature golf and other facilities. The **Gyllyngdune Gardens** are one of Falmouth's surprises for the matter-of-fact entrance gives no hint

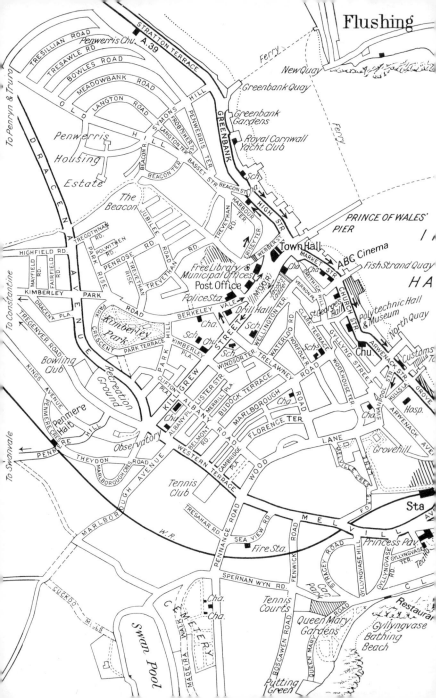

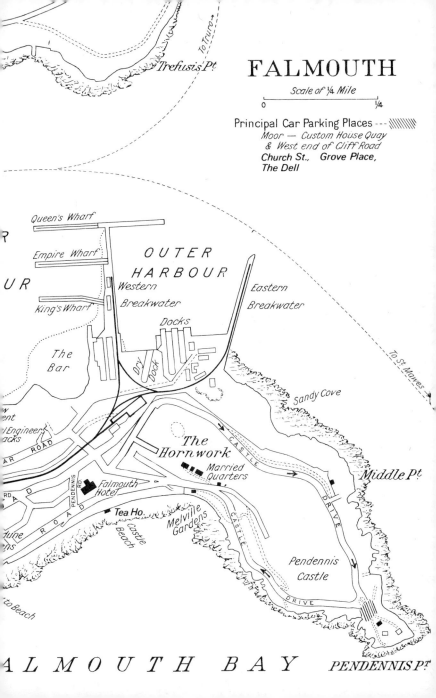

of the luxuriance of the vegetation within, much of which is of tropical origin. **Kimberley Park** is a fine 7-acre expanse of open grass and park land. The little beach at **Swanpool** farther round the bay is popular. There is a large car park, boating lake and refreshment places.

Though its streets are narrow and very full of traffic during the season, and though it has few buildings with any architectural pretensions, Falmouth town is full of interest. Walking along the busy main street (one-way traffic from High Street to the Custom House), which under various names runs within a few yards of the water from Greenbank to the vicinity of the Outer Harbour docks, one is frequently surprised by glimpses, through doorways or between buildings, of the Harbour and its multifarious shipping. Many of the shops, too, are of a kind unfamiliar to those coming from inland cities, and generally one has that satisfying sensation of being in a place which is different. The traffic centre of Falmouth is the large open space known as **The Moor,** formerly a marsh, where, within memory, snipe and wild-fowl were shot. Here is the terminus of most of the bus and coach routes, and a handy car park.

At the foot of The Moor are the Municipal Buildings, the Police Court and County Court (occupying the old Town Hall) and a large block housing the **Municipal Offices** and **Council Chamber** and the **Public Library.**

The hillside opposite the Post Office is scaled by a precipitous flight of 111 stone steps, called **Jacob's Ladder.** Those who climb the northern side of the valley should visit **Beacon Hill** for the sake of the view.

Near the foot of The Moor is the **Prince of Wales Pier,** from which most of the excursion steamers start and several of the ferries. Though intended as a landing stage rather than a promenade pier, it is a fine point from which to enjoy the ever-changing views of the Harbour.

A curiosity at the entrance to the **Custom House Quay** is *The King's Pipe*, a furnace and chimney in which excise officers used to burn contraband tobacco. Beyond this point the road becomes open on the east, and one has more frequent glimpses of the life of the Harbour.

In a small enclosure is the **Killigrew Monument,** erected by Martin Killigrew in 1737, and recalling the ancient family for so many hundred years closely identified with the fortunes of Falmouth. The Killigrews lived at **Arwenack House,** across the road.

The Docks. Docks are seldom beautiful and those at Falmouth must perforce be regarded from a utilitarian standpoint. They were first inaugurated in 1860 since when many alterations and additions have been made.

The promontory known as Pendennis Point divides the Harbour from the Bay. On the summit about 200 feet above sea level stands **Pendennis Castle** (*March and October, weekdays 9.30–5.30, Sunday 2–5.30; April, daily 9.30–5.30; May to September, daily 9.30–7; November to February, weekdays 9.30–4, Sunday 2–4; charge*). Henry VIII followed the example of several predecessors when, about 1543, he built the nucleus of the present Castle on the site of an ancient fort. The King's scheme of defence included Pendennis and St Mawes Castles, a castle at Trefusis Point, and another between Gyllyngdune and Gyllyngvase, but the last two were not built.

Though Falmouth was so far from the principal centres of activity in the Civil War, Pendennis has a notable record in connection with the strife. In 1644 Queen Henrietta Maria embarked from Pendennis for France. Prince Charles, driven westward to Bristol, and then on to Barnstaple, left Devon for Cornwall in 1645, finding refuge at Pendennis. He soon fled to Scilly. In March 1646 the Castle was besieged, both by land and sea, by the forces of the Parliament, commanded by Colonel Fortescue and Captain Batten. It was ably and stubbornly defended by Sir John Arundell, a veteran of seventy years. The siege lasted five months and the defenders surrendered on very favourable terms.

The building, which is in the care of the Department of the Environment, makes a very fine viewpoint—over Falmouth to the hilly country towards Redruth and Helston and far down the eastern coast of the Lizard and over the Harbour far out to sea. Almost due east from Pendennis Point is the white lighthouse at St Anthony, to the left of which are St Mawes and the Percuil River, while away to the north-west extends the lovely Fal.

Castle Drive is a most beautiful road skirting the Bay on one side and the Harbour on the other. Along the Drive and around the Head are attractive rose gardens.

Falmouth Harbour and the Fal

Falmouth Harbour, the estuary of the river Fal, occupies an area of approximately 10 square miles and is one of the largest havens in the Commonwealth. The entrance from the sea is stately and imposing. On the west is the bold promontory of **Pendennis,** 200 feet high, crowned with Pendennis Castle. To the east is **St Anthony Head,** 240 feet high, with the gleaming white Lighthouse at its foot, and then, just beyond the pretty estuary of the Percuil River comes St Mawes with its castle.

The municipal authorities of Truro once exercised jurisdiction over the whole of Falmouth Harbour, a privilege said to have been granted by King John long before Falmouth (or Smithicke) was thought of. In 1703 the validity of this ancient grant was contested, and Falmouth was declared to have undisputed sway over its own harbour. The Falmouth Harbour Commissioners, formed in 1870, have jurisdiction over the broad waters of the Carrick Roads as far as an imaginary line drawn from two posts north of Messack Point to an obelisk on the opposite shore. In Falmouth Bay their authority extends as far south as Rosemullion Point.

A Cruise Round the Harbour is the favourite and the most enjoyable way of obtaining some idea of this noble expanse. Motor boats are available. The ferry boats linking Falmouth with Flushing, St Mawes and other points afford opportunities for picnics and a closer examination of certain points than is possible in the course of a cruise. The Inner Harbour and docks are usually crowded with craft of all shapes and sizes, British and foreign.

The visitor may notice that many fishing boats and similar small vessels, to be seen in and about the Harbour, have big, white letters painted on their bows, followed by numbers. The letters indicate the port at which the vessel is registered and the figures the official number of the craft. Registration letters for Cornish ports are: FH = Falmouth, SS = St Ives, PW = Padstow, PZ = Penzance, FW = Fowey, TO = Truro.

We soon face the sea, and cross the wide harbour-mouth to St Anthony. Half-way across is the **Black Rock,** covered at high tide. For many years the Killigrew family were under obligation to keep fixed thereon a tall pole. Later this duty devolved on the parish church which received a due of a shilling from every ship entering the port to pay the expense of upkeep. In 1835, however, Trinity House built on the rock the granite cone, and set up the vertical iron standard and ball, which has a height of 36 feet. A vague tradition has it that the Phoenicians first bartered for Cornish tin on this rock.

The white **St Anthony Lighthouse** makes a striking contrast with the mass of black rock and green hills behind.

Northward of the lighthouse the wide mouth of the Percuil River at St Mawes opens out, with the sunny little town of **St Mawes** on the farther side, its Castle trying to look as important as it was in the time of Henry VIII. About a mile up the winding river forming St Mawes Harbour is **Percuil,** a pretty hamlet to which the ferries run. The wide extent of water between St Mawes and Pill Point (over 3 miles long by 1¼ miles wide) is known as the **Carrick Roads,** where large vessels can always find a deep and safe anchorage at all states of the tide.

St Just Pool, not very extensive, but with charmingly wooded scenery, is on our right, and a prettier little creek could hardly be conceived.

The Harbour hereabouts looks like a vast lake, with **Feock** and Porthgwidden charmingly placed among trees near the north-west shore. Away to the right, as we turn to pass down the western side, the Fal flows out from between the beautifully-wooded hills. Restronguet Point overlooks the entrance to **Restronguet Creek,** a delightful spot, extending a long distance, and including in its northern corner **Penpoll Creek** and, to the north-west, the once busy little port of **Devoran.** Boating parties should keep a keen eye on tide and channel, as there is not much water here at low tide. A mile farther south is **Mylor Creek** (between the trees we can distinguish Mylor Church, close to the water); and then as **Trefusis Point** is rounded Falmouth comes fully into view. On the right is the **Penryn River,** a branch of the Harbour extending for 3 miles to Penryn. Sheltering snugly under Trefusis is the little town of **Flushing,** one of the most sheltered corners in England.

The River Fal. Boat trips up the Fal are among the most popular excursions from Falmouth. The beauty of the river with its countless lovely creeks cannot be fully appreciated from a fast-moving motor-boat. It is essentially a waterway in which to 'potter', though the tides must be carefully watched, especially in the creeks. Here we can indicate only the features of special interest between Carrick Broads and Truro.

Straight ahead from where the river narrows is **Trelissick** with beautiful gardens and woodland walks beside the Fal (*grounds only, March to October, weekdays 11–6, Sunday 2–6; charge*).

The waters narrow further and we are in the most beautiful stretch of the river. **King Harry Passage** is lovely at all times. A car ferry connects the roads on the two banks. Various little creeks lead off on the left. The arm on the right is the Fal, navigable for 3 miles to Ruan. Between the Fal and the Truro River is Lord Falmouth's estate Tregothnan.

Continuing by the Truro River, in about 2 miles we reach the *Park Hotel* at **Malpas** (pronounced Mopus). The Tresillian River branches to the right, and here at certain states of the tide the boats turn back and passengers for Truro land at Malpas and complete the journey (2 miles) by bus or afoot. If the tide serves, however, the vessels go up to the centre of the city, providing one of the best distant views of the Cathedral. The last part of the course is very tortuous.

Excursions from Falmouth

I. To Flushing and Mylor

A circular walk of about 4 miles, which is a good introduction to characteristic Fal scenery. Reached by ferry from Prince of Wales Pier, **Flushing** is a warm and sunny little village. Dutch families founded a small settlement here in the seventeenth century, calling it Flushing after the Dutch port of that name. During the stirring and flourishing days when the Falmouth Packets were in operation, the quay was gay with the uniforms of the officers, many of whom, with their wives and families, resided in this pleasant and rather select corner of Falmouth Harbour. Today, Flushing has lapsed into a quiet and dignified riverside village with fine views across the Harbour and strong claims as a centre for grand walks in all directions. The main inner quay is used by ferries plying to and from Falmouth. Close to the door of St Peter's Church is the remnant of a Cornish cross. At **Little Falmouth,** to the north of Flushing, several of the packets were built.

Turn to the right on leaving Flushing quay, the road leading pleasantly round, past a few private houses, and so to the woods of **Trefusis** or to the beach to the right.

Cars are not allowed to continue beyond the houses, but the footpath continues right round the point, northward through the fields (or there is a shorter approach straight up through Flushing village and across the fields) to **Mylor,** once the site of a royal dockyard, the smallest in Great Britain, now in use as a boat repair yard and yacht harbour. It is a most peaceful hamlet.

Beside the south door of **Mylor Church** is the largest and tallest Cornish cross extant, said originally to have marked the grave of St Mylor himself. It was discovered in 1870, head downward, serving as a prop for the south wall of the church. It is a monolith of granite, 17 feet 6 inches high, with a round head. The present position does not set off its height to advantage, as the lower portion is embedded 7 feet. Notice the fine Norman doorways, one in the north wall of the church, the other on the west side, and the thirteenth-century carving of the Crucifixion in the outer recess on the north side of the chancel. The font is thirteenth century; the pulpit Elizabethan.

Flushing may be regained by the road above the west gate of the churchyard, or there is a more pleasant path across the fields, to the left of the road.

II. To Swanpool, Mawnan and Helford Passage

From Gyllyngvase Beach go westward by Spernan Wyn Road and keep straight on at cross-roads, shortly descending past the cemetery to **Swanpool** lake and beach. The reed-fringed pool is separated from the sea only by the road, and the very popular beach is of shingle and sand. For Maenporth continue past Swanpool and turn left at Golden Bank cross-roads beyond the golf links. **Maenporth,** a pretty sandy little cove with cliffs worn into caves and arches, together with an underground stream which flows on to the beach, is a popular picnic resort.

About 1 mile beyond Maenporth turn left for the church of **Mawnan,** delightfully situated at the mouth of the Helford River with extensive views. Note the fourteenth-century north aisle windows, the remains of the painted rood-screen and the fifteenth-century font.

From Mawnan Smith, a mile north-west, a road goes via the hamlet of Trebah, to **Helford Passage,** with its pleasant little beach beside the Helford River which is popular with boating and fishing folk. Those with an explorative nature should turn down some of the lanes in this lovely corner—that to **Durgan,** for example (on left, a mile short of Helford Passage), passes through woods overhanging the estuary and suddenly and most charmingly reveals the little hamlet at the foot of the wooded cliffs. There is a pedestrian ferry between Helford Passage and Helford during the summer.

III. To St Budock Church and Penjerrick

This, the mother church of Falmouth, lies about 2 miles to the west. Follow Tregenver Road, by the side of the Recreation Ground, for a hundred yards, then go down the hill on the left past the suburb at Swan-vale. Then take a pathway on the right across the fields up to **St Budock Church,** on the hill. There are several alternative paths. It is a pleasant round to go to Budock *via* Swanpool, and back by the field-path which abuts on Trescobeas road.

The church, with its ancient screen (restored), bespeaks its age. Note the painted panels representing saints. The brass of John Killigrew, of Arwenack (died 1567) is good. There are effigies of John Killigrew and his wife, and a monument to Sir Nicholas Parker (1619). The church has Georgian box pews.

About 1 mile to the south lie the lovely grounds of **Penjerrick** (*Sunday and Wednesday afternoons, free*). The gardens have been laid out with a cunning art that conceals art, and the view down the valley to the sea is glorious. Each shrub and plant is of interest either for its size, its luxuriance of growth, its unusual flowering capability, or its acclimatization in England. The collection of rhododendrons, azaleas and camellias are particularly fine in spring.

IV. To Constantine

This large parish, about 7 miles south-west of Falmouth just to the left of the B3291, is one of the prettiest in Cornwall. **Constantine** is close to the head of the lovely Helford River, loftily placed on granite hills and surrounded by beautiful valleys, woods and streams. The diversity of the scenery gives a special charm to the neighbourhood. We can tread a furze-covered moor one moment, and stand on rocks overlooking a huge granite quarry the next, with nothing in sight but mammoth blocks of squared granite and heaps of waste. From this scene two minutes suffice to bring us to a woody glen, through which a stream babbles noisily until it reaches a broader, unimpeded course.

The fifteenth-century **Church,** dedicated to St Constantine, is of fine proportions and has a magnificent tower. In 1958, the three old bells of the church were augmented by three more to provide for the first time in its history a fine peal of six. There are some noteworthy brasses and monuments, including a large brass to the memory of Richard Gerveys and Jane (Trefusys) his wife, with their effigies, plus eight boys on one side and eight girls on the other.

Pixie's Hall, ½ mile north of Constantine, is an Iron Age fogou, probably used for storage. The subterranean passage just opposite the house called Trewardreva, is 66 feet long, about 6 feet high and 5 feet wide. Traces of the rampart that surrounded it may be seen to the east.

The Lizard

The Lizard Peninsula is a tableland over 300 feet above sea level. In spring and summer the surface is covered with gorse, heather and other rarer plants. In 1962 a micro-wave satellite tracking station was installed in the central section, known as Goonhilly Downs. Lizard Point is the southern extremity of England, and noted for its dangerous reefs and beautiful coastal scenery.

Gunwalloe overlooks Mount's Bay. The village stands some way inland but the church is romantically situated and sheltered behind a cliff. Caves serve as bell towers and one of the bells dates from 1480. According to tradition, the church was built in the thirteenth century as a thanks-offering by a survivor of a ship wrecked at Gunwalloe. There

The thirteenth-century church at Gunwalloe Cove

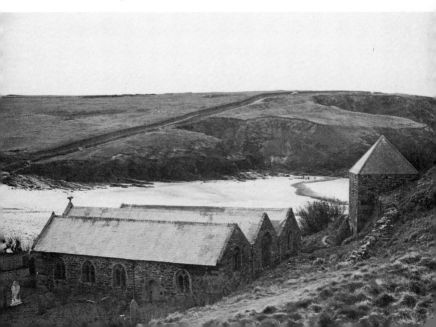

was, however, a church here long before which served as the memorial chapel of the former great manor of Winnianton. The interior contains much of interest, notably two painted panels of the old fifteenth-century rood-screen. Note the font (recently restored) and the wagon roofs of the south porch and south aisle. The separate tower belongs to an earlier church.

About $1\frac{1}{2}$ miles inland is **Cury** which has an interesting church. Particularly notable are the Norman south door, the squint connecting the south transept and chancel and the rood-loft stairways.

The road from Helston does not continue beyond Gunwalloe church, a belt of sand and a stream preventing passage for cars. The best course for those who wish to see Poldhu and Mullion as well as Gunwalloe is to continue along the Lizard road to the *Wheel Inn*, and take the turning for Cury and Poldhu. After passing the Mullion golf links this road reaches the bridge at the head of Poldhu Cove. Cross the bridge for Mullion; but for Gunwalloe climb the hill on the north side of the cove, the road coming out on the seaward side of the golf links. *Do not drive downhill* towards Gunwalloe, as cliff falls make the road dangerous and in any case one would land on soft sands. The car should be left at the top of the hill and Gunwalloe church visited on foot.

The cliff path from Gunwalloe rises steeply and as steeply falls to **Poldhu Cove** (*Poldhu*), overlooked by a large hotel. Poldhu became famous as the site of the Marconi Wireless Telegraphy Station from which the first experimental trans-Atlantic morse signals were sent and received. It was from this station, too, that successful tests were made between Poldhu and Sydney on a wavelength of 100 metres and a power of 30 kilowatts—tests which did much to direct attention to the possibilities of short-wave 'beam' wireless. The station has been dismantled, but a monument recalls the association of the place with Marconi.

The cliff path passes the *Poldhu Hotel* above the cove on Poldhu Point, and then descends into a narrow valley with a number of bungalows. Beyond is **Polurrian Cove** (*Polurrian*) with a pleasant beach. The path continues to Mullion Cove.

Mullion village, 1 mile inland from Poldhu, has many natural attractions which make it a good touring centre, including a golf course. There are a number of modern hotels on the cliffs by the famous cove. The church was rebuilt in 1500 but there are remains of thirteenth-century work in the chancel and tower. The bench-ends are extremely fine bearing many motifs including the Instruments of the Passion, a jester and a monk. The font dates from the thirteenth century.

From the village a good road runs down beside a combe for a mile, ending in **Mullion Cove** (*Mullion Cove*). This is a delightful spot at whatever state of tide it is visited, though it should be seen at least twice—at low tide and at high tide in a south-westerly wind, when the waves hurl themselves against the harbour wall and throw up immense clouds of spray. The scenery contrasts strongly with that at Kynance only a few miles south. Above rise on all sides hoary, lichen-covered cliffs, rocks piled on rocks, vaulted, tunnelled, ribbed and groined, with chasms and natural arches, like the ruins of some vast cathedral. At low tide a good stretch of sand affords safe and enjoyable bathing. On a fine day the view seawards, with **Mullion Island** across the blue water, is one of imposing grandeur, yet clothed with a soft beauty.

Mullion to Lizard Town by the Coast Path

This walk includes the cream of the Lizard coast scenery. The distance on the map is about 6 miles, but in view of the succession of steep hills few walkers will make the journey in less than 2½ to 3 hours. From Mullion Cove the path climbs steeply, with precipitous cliffs on the right, and over a majestic deep blue or dark green sea is a magnificent panorama of Mount's Bay.

At **Pradanack Head** (256 feet), the serpentine rock is noticeable. Several coves follow in succession, with sandy strips at the bottom of the black rocks, and bright yellow lichen covering the heights. *Frequent cliff falls make it unwise to venture too near the cliff edge.*

Vellan Head is next reached, and then amid impressive scenery we descend into **Gue-Graze,** noted for its soapstone. The special quality of this rock was discovered in 1755 and it was extensively quarried by the Worcester Porcelain Company. The disused quarry will be seen on the right.

The scenery here is grand and awe-inspiring. Beyond Gue-Graze is **Pigeon Ogo,** or Hugo, a fearful little cove with perpendicular cliffs 200 feet high. Then comes the **Horse,** which juts some distance seawards. From **Rill Head,** the next promontory, we look across to the Lizard, and a long winding path brings us down to far-famed Kynance.

Kynance Cove

Access by car is by a toll road which leaves the main Helston road less than 1 mile north of Lizard Town. In 1½ miles this leads to the extensive car park and tea rooms within a few hundred yards of the top of the cove.

Viewed either from the cliffs or from the path leading down, Kynance is entrancing. But to appreciate fully its grandeur, it is essential to descend to the firm sands at low tide. The way is clear, the path not very steep nor particularly 'heady', and there are easier ways for those inclined to dizziness. Most of the beach is uncovered for nearly five hours (roughly 2½ hours before and after low tide) twice every lunar day, in normal conditions. Before visiting Kynance readers are advised to ascertain time of low water on the day of the proposed visit and to arrange arrival 2½ hours earlier.

There are many items of interest at this delicious spot. The view seawards is divided by **Asparagus Island,** connected with the mainland at low water by a beach of fine sand. Immediately south of Asparagus Island and separated from it by a narrowing channel is the lengthy **Gull Rock,** often thought to be part of the island.

Midway between the rocks and Asparagus Island rises, with perpendicular sides, the huge **Steeple Rock,** so prominent a feature of Kynance views. From the sands, the charming double view of the sea, with the wonderful colours of the rocks themselves, makes one realize that there is no other place quite so lovely as Kynance.

For the caves, turn to the right. The first is termed the **Kitchen,** but no sanded kitchen floor ever approached this for whiteness. We can now closely examine the wonderful serpentine rock, for Kynance is entirely composed of this brilliant-hued stone. The polished surface is slippery and care needs to be exercised in climbing or stepping on it.

The next cave is the **Parlour,** with a superb 'bay' window. By a slight scramble over the rocks we reach the **Ladies' Bathing Pool**—small sequestered, and perfectly safe at all stages of the tide. Crossing the sands to Asparagus Island (passing the Sugar Loaf and Steeple) we mount the rocks a little way to inspect a wonderful sport of Nature, the **Devil's Letter Box** and Bellows. Owing to crevices in the rocks, and the undermining of Asparagus Island, the water is forced with stupendous power through a small vent. This is accompanied by a roar like the discharge of artillery, and a heavy shower of spray, of which the visitor must beware.

Returning to the sands, the **Drawing-Room** is close at hand, composed of beautiful green serpentine. Notice, beyond, the silhouette of the detached rocks looking seawards. On either side of the **Bishop's Rock** the outline of a face is easily discernible. High above Bishop's

Rock will be noticed a great cavity, the **Devil's Mouth,** the one dangerous spot at Kynance.

Even those unable to walk all the way from Mullion to the Lizard should find time for that onward from Kynance. **Tor Balk,** the first cliff to be surmounted, rewards us with enchanting views of the delicious cove. Next comes **Yellow Carn Head,** with the **Lion Rock** below. Eighty acres of Lizard Downs including the eastern side of Kynance Cove are in the care of the National Trust. From Pentreath Beach, beyond Yellow Carn, a rough lane leads to Lizard Town, but it is well worth while to keep to the increasingly rugged coast.

Lizard Town (*Housel Bay, Lizard*) is a medium-sized straggling and somewhat plain village having a few good hotels and a number of boarding-houses. Almost every other cottage or hut is a miniature 'Serpentine Works' where the far-famed and beautifully coloured and mottle serpentine rock is cut, polished and made into many useful and ornamental articles, including: ashtrays, necklaces, serviette rings, model lighthouses, candlesticks, clock cases and lamp standards. The 'town' is half a mile inland from Lizard Head, east of which is the site of—

Lizard Lighthouse (*open weekday afternoons*). A visit to this famous lighthouse is of more than usual interest, because of the deadly nature of the headland and its unique position on the most southerly spot in England. The lighthouse was erected in 1752, but altered in 1903. There were formerly what are known as 'twin lights', one at either end of the buildings, each with fixed white lights. A white flashing electric light of 4 million candle-power, one of the most powerful in the world, is now projected from the eastern tower only.

Polpeor Cove immediately west of Lizard Point was formerly a station of the Lifeboat service, but the boat is now stationed at Kilcobben to the east of Landewednack church.

East of the Point is the inlet of **Housel Bay,** protected on its far side by Penolver Point, a grandly piled rocky headland. The bay has a good bathing beach and is only about 8 minutes' walk from Lizard Town.

Landewednack Church. About half a mile east of Lizard Town, this is the most southerly church in England. A late Norman doorway surrounds a Perpendicular doorway. At the angle of the south chapel and chancel is a hagioscope. The font dates from 1414, and bears the inscription 'Ric. Bolham Me Fecit'. The stone-groined porch dates from 1300.

Reached from the church by a rough lane is **Church Cove.** The rock scenery here is magnificent.

The East Coast of the Lizard

Though perhaps less spectacular than the west coast, the east coast of the Lizard will suit walkers who like to get off the beaten track for with the exception of Cadgwith and Coverack there are no rivals to the popularity of Kynance and Mullion.

Starting from Church Cove we mount **The Balk,** with its tall daymark. In Polbarrow Bay is an old disused pilchard 'cellar'. **Carnbarrow** is a fine natural archway. **Ravens Hugo** and **Dollar Hugo** are impressive caves (serpentine), and should be visited by boat from Cadgwith. Just before reaching Cadgwith, and where the path turns off to the left, is the **Devil's Frying Pan.** This, too, should be inspected by boat from Cadgwith. Formerly it was a cave, but the roof fell in, and the constant washing of the sea has resulted in a curious cliff formation.

Cadgwith. Although one of the lesser-known Cornish coves by reason of its inaccessibility, **Cadgwith Cove** is amongst the most picturesque to be found anywhere in the Duchy. The approach, after leaving Ruan Minor, is down a winding, very steep and narrow lane which

Cadgwith Cove

brings the visitor quite suddenly to the miniature cove, with its thatched-roof, stone-built cottages. The two small beaches are separated by 'The Todden', a diminutive headland leading to a secluded natural bathing pool amongst the rocks.

Cadgwith lies at the mouth of a pretty, well-wooded valley and is a small and very compact little village tucked neatly between high, rocky headlands and completely unspoiled by the march of time. The local fishermen do a thriving business in crabs and lobsters.

Ruan Minor, from which the narrow, winding lane descends to Cadgwith, is a passably pretty village. The little church was formerly smaller still, for the north aisle and creeper-covered tower were added in the fifteenth century. It contains a Norman font.

A mile north of Cadgwith lies the charming hamlet of **Poltescu.** The rocky gorge (it is hardly a valley) is picturesque in the extreme. Huge boulders divert the stream into cascades as it flows to the sea at **Carleon Cove.** Formerly Poltescu was famed for its serpentine quarries and works; the old buildings remain.

From Poltesco there is a beautiful cliff path to the pleasantly situated **Kennack Sands** (car park, caravan sites), a quiet and peaceful spot amid rural surroundings, which offers good bathing.

A walk of 2½ miles along bold cliffs brings us to Black Head, passing two headlands, off which are set the rocky groups of **Carrick Luz** and **Pedn Boar.** It is a stiff climb up to **Black Head** (230 feet high), the most important promontory between the Lizard and Falmouth and a fine viewpoint.

In another mile we pass **Porthbeer Cove** and **Chynhalls Point** and drop down by way of **Perprean Cove** to the quaint and picturesque village of **Coverack** (*Coverack Headland*). This is a typical Cornish fishing village, complete with stone-built whitewashed cottages, a miniature harbour and a lifeboat station. Modern settlement has not detracted from the picturesqueness of the old village. Hotels and boarding houses cater for the increasing numbers of people visiting this charming place.

The coastal path continues by way of **Lowland Point** (National Trust) past the dangerous reef called the Manacles to **Porthoustock,** a tiny fishing village, situated in a cove between steep hills. Vessels call here and ship stone from the St Keverne quarry works, which scar the cliffs on either side of the cove. Much of this material is in the form of 'chippings' and 'fine granite' for reinforced concrete piles and works. A good deal of 'road metal' is also shipped from here.

A pleasant path through a lush valley with tropical and subtropical plants leads to **St Keverne,** which may also be reached from Coverack by the B3294 road. This is an interesting village which forms a good headquarters for those exploring the eastern coast of the Lizard; to the north the scenery is wooded and very undulating; to the west lie the vast heathery expanses of Goonhilly with the great Post Office satellite tracking station.

The fine old church, which was re-dedicated to St Keverne in 1266, has undergone many alterations. There are three sets of rood stairs, indicating that the building was extended eastward at least twice. The tower, 60 feet high, is surmounted by a spire of 38 feet, and is a familiar landmark to passing vessels on account of its proximity to the dreaded Manacles. The bench-ends are well worth careful examination. In the south-west corner is a curiosity in 'The Gudgeon from H.M. Brig o' War *Primrose*,' lost on the Manacles in 1809. More than four hundred victims of the rocks are buried in the churchyard, from which there is a magnificent view over Falmouth Bay.

From Porthoustock the coast path leads to **Porthallow,** a pleasantly situated, unspoiled village backed by steep wooded hills and complete with a wide beach. **Nare Point** lies just over a mile to the north with lovely views and shortly we reach **Gillan Creek.** There is no ferry from Gillan (*Tregildry*) but during the summer a boat from St Anthony may pull across and so save a mile or two. Otherwise continue to **Carne** at the head of the creek and almost immediately turn right along a charming road running through trees overlooking the creek to **St Anthony-in-Meneage.**

It would be hard to conceive a greater contrast to the stern, relentless Lizard cliffs than this sweet spot, hidden among trees at the extremity of Dennis Head. St Anthony Church, according to tradition, was erected as a votive offering, soon after the Conquest, by certain Normans of rank, who were storm-driven against the Cornish coast. The ship brought its living freight in safety to Gillan Creek. The church contains an Early English window in the chancel, and Perpendicular architecture, but there are no Norman remains. The thirteenth-century inscribed font is interesting, and there is a holy-water stoup of the same period.

About 1½ miles west of St Anthony is **Manaccan,** a village built high on a hill overlooking the head of Gillan Creek amid charming scenery. The church contains some Norman work but is best known for the ancient fig tree growing out of the south wall near the tower which has been there for at least two hundred years. The valley walk beside Durra is exceptionally lovely.

Helford village a mile to the north straddles the creek and is an idyllic spot in a beautifully wooded combe. The road continues round the creek to the right and ends at the *Shipwright's Arms*. At all times, Helford is very beautiful, but it is at its best at high water any June morning, when every other cottage is bedecked with roses of varying shades. A **Pedestrian Ferry** runs on request daily to the *Ferry Boat Inn* at **Helford Passage** across the estuary.

Return to Manaccan and take the road to the west which leads in 4 miles to **Mawgan,** also known as Mawgan-in-Meneage to distinguish it from St Mawgan-in-Pydar. The thirteenth-century church is mainly Perpendicular, the chancel and south transept being Decorated. The nave, north aisle and transepts have fifteenth-century wagon roofs, some elaborately carved. On the north side is a turret with rood-loft stairs and on the south an unusually wide hagioscope, or squint, with a slender supporting column. There are several interesting memorials.

A delightfully wooded road leads the 2 miles from Mawgan to **Gweek,** a village at the head of a creek of the River Helford. There is a quiet little harbour where coal is still discharged, but in the fourteenth century this was the port of Helston, since the river is tidal up to this point. The **Seal Sanctuary** at Gweek (*May to October, daily 10–9, weekends in winter; charge*) consists of three hospital pools on the banks of the Helford where seals, birds, porpoises, dolphins and turtles washed up on the Cornish coast are cared for.

Falmouth, 9 miles north-east of Gweek, is reached by the B3291.

Roseland

Roseland is the name given to the charming country bordering the eastern side of Carrick Roads, bounded roughly on the north by the River Fal from Ruan and extending southwards to the tip of the peninsula at Zone Point. The name Roseland has no origin in roses but is a later form of 'Rosinis' meaning 'moorland isle' and Roseland very nearly is an island. Far from railways and with numerous winding creeks tending to isolate little districts still more both from each other and from the outside world, it is a splendid area for walkers and for those motorists who are not averse to narrow, winding lanes. The two chief centres of population are St Mawes and Porthscatho; but almost equally popular are the various little hamlets, and during the season accommodation is usually rather difficult to obtain.

Despite a proliferation of camp sites, caravan parks and bed and breakfast signs, the area has great charm and an increasing popularity. Skin-diving, water-skiing and motor-boating are great attractions from the beaches.

The narrow promontory facing St Mawes and terminating in Zone Point is well worth exploration. Boats from Falmouth call at St Mawes and cross to the little landing-place opposite *Place Manor Hotel*, which as a charmingly situated mansion was built by Admiral Spry over the remains of a priory.

The Church of **St Anthony-in-Roseland** contains some fine examples of Early English architecture. The south door has a Norman arch, and the nave is also mainly Norman. The Lighthouse (¾ mile) may be visited on weekday afternoons, and a little distance to the north of it is a small bathing beach.

The cliffs above the Lighthouse are in the care of the National Trust (*car park*), and can be followed eastwards to Porthscatho, passing two small beaches, Porthbeor and Towan (*car park*), reached respectively from Bohortha and Porth Farm. The road, however, is very pretty and has at least equal claim. It joins the road up from Percuil a little short of **Gerrans** (*Royal Standard Inn*), a pleasant village with good views over Gull Rock and Nare Head. The church was practically rebuilt in 1848. The font is Norman; the granite piers supporting the arches are fifteenth century.

St Mawes (*Green Lantern, Idle Rocks, Manor House, Rising Sun, St Mawes, Tresanton*), on the western shore of the promontory, with a ferry service to Falmouth, may be regarded as the 'capital' of Roseland. Built up in terraces rising from the Harbour, the situation of this little port, holiday resort and former Parliamentary borough, is undeniably fine, and it is not surprising that the place is flourishing. It is well protected from both north and south, has a splendid view of the mouth of Falmouth Harbour and of the open sea, and enjoys the maximum of sunshine. It is a grand place for sailing and boating with the small Percuil River inviting excursions.

St Mawes Castle (*March and October, weekdays 9.30–5.30, Sunday 2–5.30; April, daily 9.30–5.30; May to September, daily 9.30–7; November to February, weekdays 9.30–4, Sunday 2–4; charge*), contemporary with Pendennis Castle across the water, is commanded by hills, and when held for Charles I could not long defy the Parliament. It was built 1540–3 as part of Henry VIII's programme of coastal defence and designed purely as an artillery fort to protect Falmouth Haven with the aid of the guns of Pendennis Castle.

St Mawes Harbour is formed by the small but pretty river which comes down from beyond Percuil, also known as Porthcuel.

Porthscatho (*Gerrans Bay, Roseland House, Rosevine*), a former fishing village, has become very popular with those who enjoy a holiday based on bathing, fishing and boating. It is rather more bracing than many places along this coast since it faces east and is not wedged in between high hills.

St Just-in-Roseland is 2 miles north of St Mawes on the western shore and is reached from Falmouth *via* the King Harry Ferry. It is a pretty village but its chief attraction is the famous churchyard and church. The chancel dates from 1261 though it has been much restored; the rest, including the tower, is basically fifteenth century. The most interesting features are the porch and windows, the carved bench ends, the fifteenth-century font and ewer, a fine brass of a priest, the double piscina and the roof carving.

The churchyard, which is visited annually by many thousands of people from all over the country, is exceptionally lovely. With its overhanging trees, sub-tropical plants and flowering shrubs it is perched, precariously, on the sides of a steep, well-wooded hill. There are two lych-gates. From that on the road above the churchyard a beautiful prospect is unfolded. The church is seen down below, beside the creek, charmingly situated amid rich green foliage, while beyond, between the trees, are glimpses of the waters of St Just Creek. The other lych-gate (sometimes missed by visitors) lies on the edge of the water, behind the church. The best time to visit this very beautiful spot is at high tide in early afternoon.

St Mawes to Mevagissey by the Cliffs

There has been considerable improvement of the cliff path immediately above St Anthony Lighthouse, thus opening the way for an almost uninterrupted cliff walk all the way to Mevagissey.

This route along the cliffs, sometimes by road, more often by rough path, should be attempted only by those used to hard walking. Various fishing villages are tucked away in narrow gorges in the cliffs, and are welcome havens of rest after a spell of arduous tramping. Buses run down to one or two of the coast villages from Truro and St Austell, but some of the services are very infrequent.

From the cliffs on either side of Porthscatho **Gerrans Bay** makes an imposing sweep, completed by Nare Head, with the Gull Rock just outside and the Dodman looming beyond. The path continues round the bay by **Pendower Beach,** nearly a mile in length.

Near the eastern end of the beach, which terminates in the conspicuous promontory of **Nare Head** (331 feet) (*National Trust*), is the *Nare Hotel*, and on high ground above is **Carne Beacon,** a mound 370 feet in circumference. According to tradition, this was the burial-place of Gerennius, Cornish saint and king (*circa* 600), whose castle and palace stood at Dingerein, an earthwork between Carne and Gerrans.

The summit of the Beacon commands, on a clear day, one of the finest panoramas of mid-Cornwall. Below it and well seen from the Veryan road, is **Ringarounds,** another ancient earthwork.

Veryan (*Elerkey House, Nare*), 1½ miles inland, is a charming Cornish village in a wooded valley. The place is noted for its 'round houses', whitewashed thatched cottages with Gothic windows. Two stand at each end of the village and one in the centre, each surmounted by a cross.

About ½ mile off Nare Head is the **Gull Rock.** From the head it is a stiff up-and-down walk of 2 miles to the delightful miniature fishing village of **Portloe** (*Lugger*) in a steep valley through which a stream flows to the sea. There is good fishing and bathing in the rocky little cove. The cliff path beyond Portloe is quite strenuous but the views are very good. We drop down to **Portholland,** a quaint place wedged between cliffs and hills.

The road, now near the cliffs, brings us to **Porthluney Cove.** With a lovely background of trees and rhododendrons at the head of the Cove is **Caerhayes Castle.** The castle is a modern replacement (1808, by Nash) of a Tudor House which belonged to the old Cornish family of Trevanion. The little Norman **Church** of St Michael Caerhayes, on the high ground behind the castle, re-dedicated in 1259, contains memorials, including the helmets of deceased warriors and a sword said to have been used by Hugh Trevanion at Bosworth.

Climbing the cliffs beyond the Cove, the path rejoins the road half a mile short of **Boswinger,** from which a very steep and narrow lane wriggles down to **Hemmick Beach,** on the western side of **Dodman Point** (373 feet), the boldest headland between Falmouth and Plymouth. On the summit is a tall granite cross which serves as a landmark and from which there is a glorious view.

In another mile we reach **Gorran Haven,** a former fishing village with a jumble of cottages now transformed into a popular resort. The little sandy beach with its stone quay is particularly pretty, being divided by an arm of cliff which not only imparts picturesqueness but affords protection from the wind. About 1¼ miles from the shore is a group of rocks called **Gwineas** or Gwinges.

Inland at Gorran the church is remarkably imposing with a 90-foot-high tower and a battlemented south porch with wagon roof.

From Gorran Haven the cliff path continues past Turbot Point and **Chapel Point** to **Portmellon,** a sort of overflow from Mevagissey, which is a mile beyond, by the road which here joins the cliffs. Above Chapel Point is **Bodrugan** associated with the famous Bodrugan's Leap. Here Sir Henry Bodrugan made his escape by leaping into a boat below, or so it is said: but the exact scene of this incident is not pointed out. For **Mevagissey,** *see* pp. 130–131.

Falmouth to St Austell

There are alternative routes for the motorist. The most enjoyable is the route by St Mawes to Veryan, and then taking the winding narrow by-roads to visit the coastal villages described in the previous section in the cliff walk to Mevagissey, thence by Pentewan and Porthpean to St Austell. Those wishing to see Truro and its cathedral, however, travel via the direct route by the A39 and where that road branches off left, keeping straight on by the A390 through Probus and Grampound to St Austell.

By the A39, Truro is reached in 11 miles.

Truro

Bowls At Kenwyn.
Buses Truro is an important centre, and buses run to Falmouth, Penzance, St Agnes and Trevaunance Cove, Perranporth, Bodmin, Liskeard, and Okehampton, St Austell, Redruth, Camborne, Portreath etc.
Cinema *Plaza*, Lemon Street.
Distances Barnstaple, 87 miles; Bodmin, 25, Falmouth, 11; London, 256;

Newquay, 16; Penzance, 27; St Austell, 14.
Early Closing Thursday.
Golf Treliske, Redruth Road.
Hotels *Brookdale, Carlton.*
Library Pydar Street.
Population 15,690.
Tennis At Boscawen Park beside the river, about a mile below the bridge.

Truro holds a place of considerable importance in the Duchy, being the headquarters of Cornwall County Council and many other county and public bodies. It is the main shopping centre for the many rural districts around. Market Day (Wednesday), sees Truro at its busiest, for then buses and cars from outlying villages bring a constant stream of folk who come not only to shop, but also to meet their friends and relatives, and to exchange the latest gossip.

There is a quiet dignity about the main thoroughfares such as **Boscawen Street** (so wide it can almost be described as a square),

arrow St Mary's Street, leading up to the Cathedral at Truro

Lemon Street and the less-known backwater of **Walsingham Place,** each with its solid-looking Georgian buildings.

Truro is also a small port. Colliers and other small vessels are often to be seen discharging alongside Lemon Quay, while from **Worth's Quay** (approached by steps from Boscawen Bridge), motor launches make the beautiful trip down the Truro River, meeting the Fal about a mile and a half below Malpas, and continuing to Falmouth Town.

A stroll round Truro will reveal many unsuspected quaint and crooked alleyways. At the side of most of these narrow little lanes there is a miniature stream, meandering along to join the Allen and Kenwyn rivers which, in turn, sidle along to swell the Truro River at the head of which the city stands.

At the top of Lemon Street is the imposing **Lander Memorial,** a Doric column erected to the memory of Richard and John Lander, who traced the river Niger to its exit to the sea in 1827.

Truro Cathedral

Truro Cathedral may not have the age-worn beauty of its easterly neighbours at Exeter and Wells, but it is an extremely interesting building for those who know the older foundations since it is one of the few cathedrals to have been built in modern times. It was raised by the united efforts of all religious denominations in a county which then was more inclined to non-conformity than to the Church. J. L. Pearson was the architect, and the style is Early English. The cloisters have still to be completed.

King Edward VII (then Prince of Wales) laid the foundation stone in 1880, and the building was consecrated by the Archbishop of Canterbury in 1887.

The Central or **Victoria Tower,** 250 feet high, forms a Cornish Memorial of Queen Victoria. The western towers, 204 feet high, completed in 1909, are known as the **Edward VII** and **Alexandra Towers.**

Internally the light-grey stone of the building and the clear glass of the nave windows leave a rather bare effect which is, however, amply compensated by the fine proportions and the richness of the reredos and the east window. The Cathedral was raised on the site of the old Parish Church of St Mary, the south aisle of which was retained to form the south aisle of the Cathedral, and here again the brightness of the nave provides a striking contrast. The aisle has the quiet charm of a beautiful old church of bygone generations. West of the south transept is the **Baptistery,** a memorial to Henry Martyn, the great Truro mis-

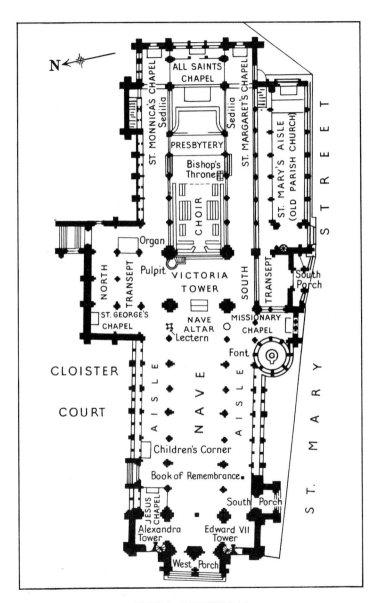

N

ALL SAINTS CHAPEL

ST. MONNICA'S CHAPEL

Sedilia

Sedilia

ST. MARGARET'S CHAPEL

PRESBYTERY

Bishop's Throne

CHOIR

ST. MARY'S AISLE (OLD PARISH CHURCH)

S T R E E T

Organ

Pulpit

NORTH TRANSEPT

SOUTH TRANSEPT

South Porch

VICTORIA TOWER

ST. GEORGE'S CHAPEL

NAVE ALTAR

Lectern

MISSIONARY CHAPEL

Font

CLOISTER

COURT

AISLE

N A V E

AISLE

S T .   M A R Y

Children's Corner

Book of Remembrance

JESUS CHAPEL

South Porch

Alexandra Tower

Edward VII Tower

West Porch

TRURO CATHEDRAL

sionary. It is an architectural gem, the stones and marbles forming a harmony of gorgeous tints. Appropriately near at hand is the *Missionary Chapel*. In the south choir aisle is the **Chapel of St Margaret of Scotland,** for the especial use of the girls of the diocese.

The **Reredos,** of richly-carved Bath stone, is of great beauty. Behind it is the **Chapel of All Saints,** open daily for prayer and meditation.

In the north choir aisle the terra-cotta group by *Tinworth*, representing 'Christ Going to Calvary', compels admiration by its beauty and dignity.

At the east end of the north choir aisle is the **Chapel of St Monica,** for the use of members of the Mothers' Union and kindred societies.

The **Jesus Chapel,** in the north-west corner, is separated from the nave and adjacent aisle by a coloured screen, which strikes a somewhat novel but by no means unpleasing note. **St George's Chapel,** in the North Transept, has been dedicated 'to the interests of boyhood'.

Under the window—the most westerly on the south side—which contains the picture of John Wesley preaching at Gwennap Pit, is the *Book of Remembrance*, containing the names of some 4,000 Cornishmen who fell in the 1914–18 War.

The Royal Institution of Cornwall was founded in 1818 and its **Museum and Art Gallery** (*November to March 10–4; April to October, 10–5; free*) is well known. Many of the Cornish prehistoric objects exhibited are of exceptional interest and include ornaments and weapons of bronze and burial urns of 'sun-baked' clay with typical ornamentation added while the clay was soft; also relics of the Stone Age. The Museum also contains an extensive collection of Cornish minerals, while the Art Gallery has a fine collection of pictures by well-known artists.

With its excellent transport services Truro is a very convenient holiday centre, situated as it is within easy reach of Falmouth, St Ives, Penzance, Fowey, etc. Nearer to hand are many pleasant walks including that along the river to Malpas, passing **Boscawen Park** with its subtropical plants, shady seats, small lake and refreshment house. There are tennis, football and cricket grounds near by.

Excursions from Truro

I. To St Clement and Malpas

St Clement is prettily situated 1½ miles east of Truro on the banks of the Tresillian River. The thirteenth-century church was virtually rebuilt in 1865 and mural paintings, benches, the old roof and nearly everything else of interest were swept away. But near the porch still stands the Ignioc Stone regarded as the finest of Cornwall's inscribed stones. The words IGNIOC VITALI FILI TORRICI may be discerned and there is also an Ogham inscription.

From St Clement it is only a mile by field-path to **Malpas,** an ancient little port at which passengers from Falmouth land when the tide is low. The views towards the Fal and along the Truro and Tresillian Rivers are enchanting.

II. To Woodbury, Coombe and Feock

Woodbury may be reached by ferry from Malpas or by taking the first turning on the left off the A39 Falmouth road immediately after crossing the old railway. It was the home of Henry Martyn, the martyr missionary whose memorial is in Truro Cathedral, and is a favourite spot for river picnics.

Coombe to the south is prettily situated in a small creek off the Fal, ½ mile north of King Harry Passage. It is a centre of the Fal oyster industry and over thirty small sailing boats dredge the main rivers and creeks for oysters during the winter.

Feock, 3 miles south of Coombe, is charmingly situated, with Restronguet Creek on one side and the broad Carrick Roads on the other. The separate tower is all that remains of the old church, the main building being Victorian. The font is late Norman and the pulpit incorporates four Flemish panels of the late sixteenth century. Above the curious lych gate, and forming part of it, is a small 'parish room'. The road north from Feock joins the B3289 which leads into the A39.

III. To Ruan Lanihorne and Tregony

St Michael Penkevil is 3½ miles south-east of Truro by the Malpas ferry or it can be reached from Tresillian on the A39 St Austell road. The church, dating from 1261, was restored by G. E. Street in 1863–5 and contains several monuments to the Boscawens (Viscounts Falmouth).

About 2 miles east of St Michael Penkevil is the little village of **Lamorran** set on the charming Lamorran Creek off the Fal. The tiny thirteenth-century church was rebuilt in 1845. The circular font is Norman and there is an impressive monument to John Verman and his wife.

Continuing westward, we arrive at **Ruan Lanihorne** at the head of the navigable section of the Fal. The fine church includes some Norman masonry and a tower built in 1675. The effigy of a priest with hands in prayer dates from the thirteenth century. Long ago the Fal penetrated well beyond Ruan Lanihorne and was navigable as far as Tregony. This was a thriving, busy town long before Penryn and Truro. There is evidence that the tide ebbed and flowed at Tregony Quay. From very early times Tregony had the right of sending two burgesses to Parliament. The ancient tin mines and later, the china clay pits were the ruin of the place, for the Fal brought down sand and rubbish from them in such quantities that the bed of the river was choked. Two Acts of Parliament, passed by Henry VIII, failed to stop the tin mining. Little by little the waters shrank from the old town, until now there is little more than a stream a few feet wide at this point and the navigable portion is more than 4 miles distant. Consequently, Tregony, situated on the slope of a steep hill, has now become a sleepy village.

Leave Truro by the A39 St Austell road which leads in 3½ miles to **Tresillian** at the head of the Tresillian River. Remains of earthworks in the area give evidence of many combats in the past. At Tresillian Bridge, in 1646, the treaty of peace was declared between Sir Ralph Hopton and Sir Thomas Fairfax by which the former's regiment of horse was to be disbanded and Truro quietly surrendered to Cromwell's representatives.

The St Austell road continues to **Probus** where the church was made collegiate by King Athelstan in 926. The glorious three-stage tower is the highest in Cornwall at more than 123 feet and is richly decorated. It was built in the time of Henry VIII in the style of Somerset towers. There are some fine houses in the neighbourhood, notably **Trewithen** a stately early Georgian house with a splendid dining room. The garden contains camellias, magnolias, rhododendrons and various rare plants (*garden: March to June and September, weekdays 2–4.30; house and garden: May to September, Thursday 2–4.30*).

In a further 2½ miles we come to the ancient town (now little more than a village) of **Grampound** on the main stream of the Fal. Like its sister Tregony it once enjoyed commercial prosperity and Parliamentary representation. Refuse from the china-clay workings farther north here gives the Fal a milky-white appearance. In the small market place is a late medieval though mutilated cross.

In a further 6 miles we arrive at—

St Austell

Bowls Poltair Recreation Ground.
Cinemas *Capitol, Classic.*
Distances Bodmin, 11 miles; Liskeard, 19; London, 242; Newquay, 16; Truro, 14.
Early Closing Thursday.
Golf St Austell Bay has two courses, at Tregongeeves and Crinnis (Carlyon Bay).
Hotels *Clifden; Cliff Head,* Carlyon Bay; *Pier House,* Charlestown; *Porth Avallen,* Carlyon Bay; *White Hart.*
Library Carlyon Road.
Population 32, 710.
Speedway Cornish Stadium, Par Moor.
Tennis Public courts at Poltair Recreation Ground; also at Crinnis and Par.

St Austell is an important business and residential town which is also a convenient touring centre for various places of interest. Many excellent and up-to-date shops in the central development attract the hundreds who camp or lodge in neighbouring villages or farms.

The by-pass skirting the southern edge of the town carries most of the through traffic, but even so congestion occurs in the main street during the holiday season.

Holy Trinity Church is one of the finest in the county, and its carvings have been described as 'an epitome of the Creed ... a Gospel addressed to the eye'. The Perpendicular tower, which rises to a height of close on 100 feet, is ornamented with niches containing statues of the Holy Trinity, the Risen Saviour, the Virgin Mary, apostles, bishops and saints, eighteen in all; besides numerous other symbols of the Christian faith. Above the western door may be seen an ancient stone clock face. This is said to be the dial of a 'clok' noted in the reign of Edward VI—the only one in Cornwall at that period. Among other exterior ornaments of the building may be noted a series of fifteen escutcheons illustrating, by emblematic changes, the Passion of Our Lord.

The church itself was rebuilt in the fifteenth century, but contains portions of the three preceding styles. The font, which stands within an ornate modern baptistery, is late Norman. A number of old carved bench-ends are preserved in frames in the ringers' chamber beneath the tower, and a portion of the old rood screen may still be seen. Above the porch is a parvise chamber which, it is thought, was used in days gone by as a resting-place for travelling monks.

At the corner of Fore Street and North Street, is the **Mengue Stone,** which formerly occupied a position where three manors met, and from various circumstances was regarded with awe. It is set near the south-west wall of the church, the position being marked by a brass tablet.

According to tradition, a reputed witch was burnt alive on the stone.

About ¼ mile out of the town, in the woods on the left-hand side of the Bodmin road, is the **Holy Well of Menacuddle** and the **Stone Chair,** said to be Druidical, rough-hewn from a piece of granite, from which the well gets its name ('menacuddle' is old Cornish for 'stone in a wood').

Southwards, at **Trewhiddle,** close to the lovely Pentewan Valley, a very important discovery of Roman and early Saxon relics was made in 1774. The hoard included an exceptionally beautiful silver chalice (said to be the oldest surviving piece of church plate), mounts for drinking horns, a silver strap-end, rings, a knotted scourge of silver wire and various other silver articles. Of priceless historical value, they are in the care of the British Museum.

A china clay pit near St Austell

The China Clay Industry. St Austell is chiefly notable as the centre of this industry. The scattered groups of giant, white pyramids seen to the north of the railway line are the 'burrows' of waste material extracted during the process of refining china clay, that pure white, velvety substance, the production of which is a principal industry of the Duchy today.

Charlestown (*Pier House*) is a tiny port which still secures by right of proximity a considerable part of the shipping business of the clay country. Its single small dock is usually busy with vessels of the smaller classes: steamships loading china clay in bulk, grimy little colliers discharging coal. It has in recent years become popular with summer visitors, especially with people staying at the nearby Duporth Holiday Camp.

Eastward from Charlestown is **Carlyon Bay,** an attractive modern suburb with hotels, golf links, excellent sands and facilities for sports and games of all kinds.

Porthpean, a mile south of St Austell, lies on a small cliff-sheltered bay and is a popular little resort, its beach being thronged with visitors in the summer. At low tide the rock pools fascinate old and young alike.

At Carthew, 2 miles north of St Austell on the A391 Bodmin road is the **Wheal Martyn Museum** (*April to October, daily 10–6; charge*). A tour of this restored clay works gives a fascinating picture of the history of Cornwall's clay mining industry.

Excursions from St Austell

I. To Mevagissey
Leave St Austell by the B3273 which leads in 3½ miles to Pentewan. The once busy harbour is now silted up and the village is now a popular resort. The expanse of turf bordering the beach is largely given over to caravan and camping sites. The beach is excellent and would be better still but for the discoloration of the sea caused by the discharge of the 'white river' as it comes down from the china clay workings. A mile or so to the north-east is Black Head on the northern side of which is **Trenarren,** a delightful little village almost lost among the trees of its lovely valley.

In a further 2 miles we arrive at—

Mevagissey

Buses Mevagissey and Pentewan are connected with St Austell by a regular bus service.

Car Parks Two in the town; one on the quay.
Hotels *Treloen, Tremarne.*
Population 2,050.

Mevagissey has grown from an old-world fishing village into a popular resort for summer visitors. Its narrow streets and devious alleyways, with cottages perched at crazy angles, remain as relics of the days when fishing and smuggling were its main activities. On the steep hillsides surrounding the ancient village numerous boarding-houses have sprung up. Pleasure boats, taking visitors for an hour's trip in the bay, ply constantly from the quays in summer.

Seats and benches on the quays of the inner harbour accommodate holiday-makers who laze in the sunshine and watch the fishing boats or pleasure-craft go in or out, while the arms of the outer harbour provide delightful promenades. Anglers occupy the pier-heads, where the catch may be mackerel, pollack, conger, with an occasional bass or turbot. During the season motor coaches run daily trips to Falmouth, Newquay, The Lizard, Fowey, Land's End, etc.

In by-gone days huge quantities of pilchards were caught in Mevagissey seines, 'cured' in rock salt, packed in casks, and exported to Italy and the West Indies. The victualling yards of the Navy also took supplies, the savoury fish being nick-named 'Mevagissey Ducks' by the seamen. The little fishing port's record output was in the year 1724, when over four thousand tons of pilchards were dispatched.

Cottages on the eastern cliff side, extending from the *Fountain Inn* to the Battery, form the most ancient part of the town, which was known as Porthilly. The churchtown was Lanmorroc. The earliest known record of Mevagissey, as a place name, occurs in 1400.

The **Parish Church,** St Peter's, stands on ground which has been consecrated for over fourteen hundred years. A Celtic 'Lan' was established here about 550, when the monk Moroch built his wattle oratory and cell, which later was succeeded by a wooden building. The first church of stone was erected about 950. This Saxon building was rebuilt about 1100 under the Norman bishop of Exeter. Again rebuilt in 1259 the church became cruciform. A north aisle was added about 1450. The final restoration in 1887 brought the church to its present state. The font is late Norman and the registers date from 1598. On the north side of the sanctuary is an interesting memorial to Otwell Hill dated 1617.

A finely cut slab in Cornish slate on the north wall commemorates the Dart family (1632).

Polstreath Beach, beyond the coastguard station, a favourite spot for safe bathing and picnics, is of fairly easy access, but involves a stiff climb to the cliff top on returning.

The best view of the Harbour and the town huddled between the hills at its head is from near the top of the Portmellon road, a sharp climb southward. **Portmellon** consists of a small colony at the edge of a pretty cove about a mile from Mevagissey; its little beach offers fair bathing.

Inland from Mevagissey are several small but attractive villages, all of them quite unspoilt. The largest is **St Ewe** whose impressive church is approached through an avenue of palms. The tower and south aisle date from the fourteenth century. The rood screen, which runs across the nave only, has some fine elaborate carving. There are also some interesting monuments.

II. To Lostwithiel

Leave St Austell by the A390 and continue along this road when the Fowey road branches right to reach **St Blazey.** The fifteenth-century church was drastically restored in the nineteenth century but there are some impressive monuments.

In a further 1½ miles a left turn leads to **Lanlivery** whose church tower, rising 97 feet, is a prominent landmark. The large octagonal font dates from the fifteenth century. The old wagon roofs have been preserved in the south aisle and south porch.

The main road continues to—

Lostwithiel

Bowls Restormel Road.
Distances Bodmin, 6 miles; Fowey, 7; London, 239; St Austell, 9; Truro, 23.
Early Closing Wednesday.

Hotels *Carotel Motel, Royal Oak, Royal Talbot.*
Population 1,905.

Although the picturesque old town is much visited, its regular clientele consists chiefly of anglers, for the 'fishfull river of Foy,' as Carew has it, is celebrated for its salmon and trout. To tourists and holiday-makers one of the most attractive features is Restormel Castle, a mile or so to the north. Between Lostwithiel station and the Church is the fine **Old Bridge** (probably fourteenth century) of five arches, with much

Lostwithiel Church, from the east

appreciated angular recesses on either side for the protection of foot-passengers.

The old **Duchy Palace** was the ancient Exchequer, Shire Hall and Stannary Prison. It dates from about 1280. The building has been restored, and is now used for Masonic purposes.

St Bartholomew's Church has a graceful octagonal spire dating from the thirteenth century and called by G. E. Street, 'the pre-eminent glory of Cornwall.' Near the south porch is a medieval cross with a fine head, restored in 1882. The font, of Pentewan stone, is remarkably carved. Close by is a carved wooden pedestal on which stands the alms-box, dated 1645. In a south window will be noticed an alabaster carving, coloured, representing the flaying of St Bartholomew. The east window is Early English work, and of unusual size: 34 feet by 14 feet.

The memorials and monuments are of much interest. Against the north wall is a brass effigy in armour representing Tristram Curteys (date 1423). Note in the outside of the south wall the two sepulchral recesses. It is supposed that here were buried Robert de Cardinham and his wife (about 1225). The parish stocks, of seven holes, are preserved in the south porch.

The **Guildhall** was erected in 1740. The Borough Regalia and In-signia are most interesting, including a Silver Mace and a Silver Oar, both of 1670. Lostwithiel is an ancient borough, its first charter having been granted in 1189. Visitors who wish to inspect the Guildhall should apply to the Municipal Offices opposite. The celebrated Silas Titus, author of *Killing noe Murder*, was M.P. for Lostwithiel, 1663–79.

A few yards below the *Talbot Hotel* is a shop bearing a curious old tablet stating that 'Walter Kendal founded this house and hath a lease for 3,000 years which had beginning Sept. 29, 1652'.

Restormel Castle (*March and October, weekdays 9.30–5.30, Sunday 2–5.30; April, daily 9.30–5.30; May to September, daily 9.30–7; November to February, weekdays 9.30–4, Sunday 2–4; charge*) is situated 1½ miles north of Lostwithiel, reached by the road next to the *Talbot Hotel*. It leads along a lovely valley, thickly wooded on the left, and affording a view of the Fowey River and the main line of the railway to the right, across the meadows. After a long mile the road turns sharply to the left, uphill, leaving extensive farm buildings on the right in the corner. The castle is now easily seen across the hill, a couple of hundred yards from the road, on the right.

The earliest castle was an earthwork consisting of a ring motte with a bailey, now largely obliterated, on the west side. This dated from the early twelfth century. About 1200 a masonry shell keep was built on top of the circular ramparts, with the curtain wall over 8 feet thick. In the late thirteenth century two-storeyed apartments surrounding the courtyard were built inside the keep, replacing earlier wooden structures.

The earliest mention is in 1264 when it was surrendered, with other castles, to Simon de Montfort by Thomas de Tracy. Since 1299 it has belonged to the Earldom (later Duchy) of Cornwall. In the sixteenth century the buildings were unoccupied and ruinous. Yet in the Civil War the keep was garrisoned by the Parliamentary army and was captured by Sir Richard Grenville on behalf of the King in 1644.

Lanhydrock House (*April to October, daily 11–1, 2–6 ; garden always open ; charge*) is situated 3½ miles north of Lostwithiel and reached by the B3268. Lanhydrock was given to the National Trust by Viscount Clifden, who lived here. The fine avenue was planted in 1648. Part of the house is of the Tudor period, but the greater part of the old mansion was destroyed by fire and rebuilt with additions in the 'eighties of last century. It stands in a park of 366 acres. The barbican, or principal entrance, is a fine battlemented structure bearing the date 1651. The picture gallery, in the original north wing, has a remarkable plaster ceiling, depicting scenes from the Old Testament. There are formal gardens, originally laid out in 1857, with a number of bronze urns from the Chateau de Bagatelle by Louise Ballin, goldsmith to Louis XIV.

The **Fowey Valley,** north of Lostwithiel, boasts some glorious scenery. The superb Valley Drive between Bodmin Road and Doublebois may be combined with a visit to Lanhydrock.

St Austell to Fowey

Leave St Austell by the A390 and in 1½ miles branch right along the A3082. **Par Sands** soon open out with a splendid marine view. At low water there is an extensive flat beach of good sand and a number of bathing huts, model-yacht pools and various games facilities attract large numbers of visitors. The harbour is small but has a flourishing and busy trade. Coal is brought and china clay, stone and granite shipped in large quantities. **Spit Beach,** west of the harbour, is a popular place for picnics.

On the hills inland stands the village of **Tywardreath.** The Manor of Tiwardrai is recorded in the Exeter Domesday. St Andrew's Priory, which stood just below the present churchyard, was founded about A.D. 1150 by monks from Angers in Normandy, but it has now disappeared. St Andrew's Church dates from 1347 and was largely rebuilt in 1880. The tower, which is original, dates from 1480.

East of Par Sands is the well-wooded, crescent-shaped cove of **Polkerris,** where a diminutive stone pier shelters a good sandy beach. At one time fishing was the predominant industry at Polkerris, and the old fish cellars remain.

On the way to Fowey is **Four Turnings** in the centre of which is an inscribed stone about 8 feet high. The defaced inscription has been read DRVSTANSI HIC JACIT CVNOWORVS FILIVS: 'Drustanus here lies the son of Cunomorus.' Drustanus is identified with Tristram and Cunomorus is one of the names of King Mark of Cornwall.

Fowey

Bathing Among rocks and at the sandy beach of Readymoney Cove.
Boating Boats for hire from Town Quay and Polruan Quay.
Bowls Squire's Field Recreation Ground.

Buses To Par, St Blazey and St Austell; to Golant, Lostwithiel, and Lerryn; from Bodinnick to Lanreath, Pelynt and Looe.
Cinema *Troy*, Fore Street.
Distances Bodmin, 12 miles; Falmouth,

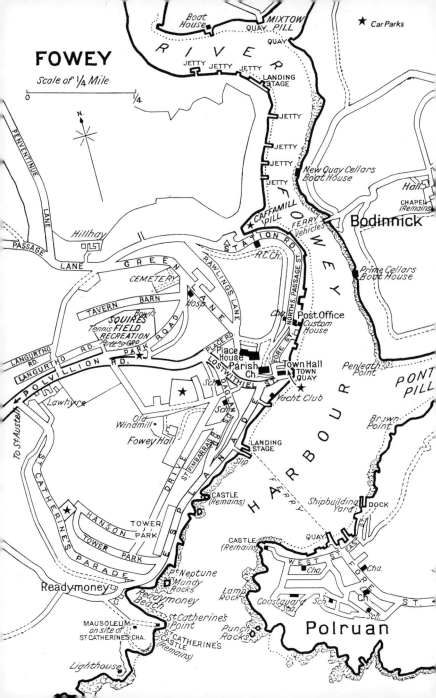

36; London, 241; Newquay, 25; St Ives, 50; Truro, 23.

Early Closing Wednesday.

Ferries There are two harbour ferries: (a) from Passage Slip to Bodinnick (car-carrying service); (b) from Whitehouse to Polruan (pedestrians only).

Fishing Pollack and whiting all the year round; mackerel and bass from June to September. Salmon fishing by net and rod. Shark fishing is also popular.

Golf Carlyon Bay Golf Club.

Hotels Ashley House, Marina, Old Quay House, Penlee, Riverside.

Library Church Avenue.

Tennis Squire's Field Recreation Ground.

Fowey is an ancient seaport, with narrow streets and houses attractively jumbled together. The harbour is a charming inlet between imposing headlands, extending inland for 6 miles to Lostwithiel, with good depth of water for the first mile or so. This strip of water provides a safe and picturesque anchorage for hundreds of yachts during the summer months. The most popular spot is the Town Quay. To its left the steep hillside at **Bodinnick** is covered from summit to water's edge in rich, dark green foliage. Opposite is the lovely wooded creek of **Pont Pill** while to the right lies picturesque **Polruan.**

The business of the port has grown somewhat of late, and those who cherish the theory that all the trade must go to the big ports will look with surprise upon the many door plates announcing the presence of Vice-Consulates of other countries. Vessels of 10,000 tons and more put into Fowey to receive cargoes of china clay for various parts of the world. The jetties at which the clay is shipped are well equipped, and those who do not mind being powdered with white dust will find interest in a visit to the jetty-side.

The **Parish Church** of St Fin Barr (Fimbarrus) of Cork is beautifully proportioned. It was rebuilt in 1336. The lofty fifteenth-century wagon roof of the nave has still much of the original carved timber. The font is Norman (1150). The south porch is rib-vaulted in stone and has a chamber above. The carved pulpit, said to have been made from the oak of a Spanish galleon, bears the date 1601. The very handsome four-staged tower, which rises to a height of 119 feet, contains a clock and a peal of eight bells.

The mansion overlooking the church is **Place House,** the seat of the Treffry family for centuries (*not open*).

The Esplanade, or cliff road, leads to the harbour mouth. This road passes Whitehouse Ferry and slip; 'The Haven', once home of Sir Arthur Quiller-Couch, the eminent novelist in whose books Fowey figures as 'Troy Town'; continues past Polly Foot's Cove to Readymoney Cove and the Battery.

Just beyond *Point Neptune*, a big house, is **Readymoney Cove,** in the hollow between the Esplanade and St Catherine's Castle. It is a pretty spot, much used for bathing.

St Catherine's Castle (*daily 9–sunset; free*), built in 1540, is now but a small ruin, though it played an important part in the defence of the harbour in the old days when raids were common between rival towns on either side of the Channel. The harbour chain was held at the blockhouses, one a little farther up the river and the other at Polruan. A lovely view of the sea coast and the surrounding district is gained from the headland in which the castle is set.

Above the gorse on this height is the **Rashleigh Mausoleum.** Two granite arches, intersecting at right angles and surmounted by a Maltese cross, span the tombs of William Rashleigh, of Menabilly (died 1871), and his wife and daughter.

Polridmouth Cove is beyond, and a little distance farther brings us to **Gribbin Head,** with its Beacon, commanding a magnificent view.

Excursions from Fowey

I. The Hall Walk and Lanteglos

Cross the harbour by the ferry to Bodinnick, beloved of artists. Go up the steep village street about 150 yards, and take the path through the gate on the right. The Hall is now a farmhouse from the vicinity of which there is a superb view across the harbour. Away beyond is the granite pillar on Gribbin Head, and in the far distance looms the Dodman.

On Hall Walk are two granite memorials, one commemorating the men of Fowey and Lanteglos who fell in the 1939–45 war and the other, on Penleath Point, in memory of Sir Arthur Quiller-Couch.

The Walk leads to a path which skirts **Pont Pill,** and presently Lanteglos Church is sighted on the other side of the creek. The path, still at the hill top, enters through a field into a private wood, though the path is public. Through the thick trees on the right glimpses can be obtained of the waters of the creek, a good distance below. The path descends to the road where turn left for an old mill. Bearing right the road continues round and back to **Pont** on the other side of the river.

From Pont it is a stiff climb to **Lanteglos Church,** an ancient building well worth a visit. Note the fine font, the carved bench-ends and panelling, the old wagon-roofs, the old glass in the east window of south aisle, the stocks and the alabaster tablet showing St Lawrence's martyr-dom. Among the tombs of interest special note should be made of two Mohun brasses. The lantern cross outside the south door can hardly be rivalled in Cornwall.

From the church a road runs westward to join the road from Pont to Polruan Quay, about 1½ miles from Lanteglos Church. The road descends steeply through the village of **Polruan**. A little way down, note the remains of an ancient cross and village well or fountain. From the quay, a motor ferry connects with Whitehouse Slip, on the Fowey side of the Harbour.

II. To Gribbin Head

A walk of about 3 miles, via the Esplanade and the path that descends into Readymoney Cove. Cross the stream and ascend by the path to the left through the woods. The ruins of St Catharine's Castle are soon reached. From this point it is possible to walk around the edge of the

Looking up the River Fowey from Polruan

cliffs to Polridmouth; but those who take this route must be prepared to cross two deep 'coombes'.

The ascent of **Gribbin Head** is not difficult. The view is grand. Westward is the long, flat-topped promontory of the Dodman. Par sands and harbour lie in the bay. Fowey Harbour is to the north-east, and in the far distance Rame Head, outside Plymouth, is discernible on a clear day.

The return can be varied by way of Menabilly Barton and so to the main road, where it is possible to pick up a bus.

III. The Luxulyan Valley

To reach this very lovely valley take the A3082 to Par, turn right along the main road to St Blazey (see page 131) and in a further ½ mile turn left to Ponts Mill. The entrance to the valley is about ¼ mile farther on. An alternative and in many ways more enjoyable route is to drive to Par station and take a train by the Newquay branch line to Luxulyan station, travelling the length of the valley.

At **Luxulyan** village we are well in the granite district, and the church is one of the finest of Cornwall's granite churches. Note the huge blocks in the tower, one 7 feet 2 inches long. The glass in the west window of the tower is sixteenth century. The pillars supporting the arches of the arcades are monoliths of granite. The roofs of the north and south aisles show remains of the original wagon roofs. The documents of the ancient Stannary Parliament were kept in the turret of this church, but during the Civil War they were taken to Lostwithiel and there destroyed.

The Roman **Well of St Cyors** should be visited. It is close to and below the village pump, and is apt to be overlooked. The tiny Gothic 'chapel' remains, but the tank in the interior was an anachronism and has been removed.

From the village there are several routes to the valley. The best and by far the easiest for a stranger to find is as follows. Beyond the *King's Arms* turn right over the railway bridge and turn right again at the top of the hill. Go right through the village, passing the church on the left and down the hill. On reaching a stone bridge over a very good trout stream, turn right, then keep straight on until the **Treffry Viaduct** is reached. The viaduct, 100 feet high and over 650 feet in length, was built, at a cost of £7,000, in 1839 to carry a railway (now closed) from the Treffry granite quarries and as an aqueduct. The view from above well repays the climb.

Take the first small turning to the left beyond the viaduct. This leads right through the valley (muddy and treacherous going after rain) to the site of the former waterfall which used to plunge 200 feet. The water is now piped underground to the clayworks. Nevertheless the climb up to the top is rewarding for the views it offers. From here we take the path leading along and down the hill to the china clay works. It is a walk of about 1½ miles to Par station.

IV. By water to Lostwithiel

A trip of about 6 miles. Starting from Whitehouse, we pass the ferry at **Bodinnick,** and as we thread our way between the many vessels loading china clay, we have a good view of the huge mechanical conveyors on the jetties. We soon have a series of delightful river vistas. On the right is the wide **Penpoll Creek,** up which at high tide one can row for a mile to **Penpoll,** from which a short climb leads to **St Veep.** The church of St Veep, reconstructed in 1336, has a fine fifteenth-century fort and some good wood carving.

On the left of the river ½ mile further up is **Golant** sheltering under a hill. The attractively situated church was consecrated in 1509 and contains much of interest despite the 'restoration' of 1842. Note the holy well beside the porch, well-preserved bench-ends incorporated into the pulpit and stalls, fifteenth-century stained glass, and fine roofs in the nave and aisle.

To the west of Golant is **Castle Dore,** an Iron Age fort said to have been the palace of King Mark, the uncle of Tristram, and a meeting place of the Knights of the Round Table. It is the reputed burial-place of Tristram and Isolde.

Cliff on the opposite side of the river is a favourite camping spot; the creek leading away to the right. Beyond Cliff is the River Lerryn which winds through beautiful woodland to the quaint village of Lerryn.

On the left, as the river continues towards Lostwithiel, stands the mansion of Penquite. In a further ½ mile on the right bank is **St Winnow** church beautifully set close to the water's edge. The building is basically of the fifteenth century though there are Norman remains. The old bench-ends are quaint and there are two sixteenth-century windows. Much of the rood screen is original work and the pulpit is well carved in an arabesque design.

Above St Winnow the river narrows considerably as it approaches Lostwithiel (see page 131).

Fowey to Looe

Take the Bodinnick ferry and continue eastwards to **Lansallos** where the fifteenth-century church has thirty-four carved bench-ends, good wagon roofs and a Norman font. From the road by the churchyard wall a lane runs down to the sea at an attractive bathing beach in **Lantivet Bay.** This land is in the care of the National Trust and the paths are well kept, but there is no way for cars.

The road heading eastwards from Lansallos leads to the hamlet of Windsor where a right turn brings us in 2 miles to—

Polperro

Bathing Bathing is possible towards high tide on a sandy shingle beach outside the pier; but a more satisfactory spot and the general resort is Chapel Pool, among the rocks on the seaward side of Peak. There are also several sandy coves at the Talland end of the cliff path.
Buses Regular services to Looe and Plymouth.

Car Parks Car parks and garages, some equipped with turntables, border the road leading down. Cars may not be parked on the roadway itself for even the briefest period.
Early Closing Saturday.
Hotel *Claremont.*

The ancient and charming village of Polperro is undoubtedly one of the most picturesque in Cornwall. In the bottom and upon the lower slopes of a narrow and precipitous winding gorge between 400 feet high cliffs are huddled the stone-built cottages of about a thousand inhabitants.

The **Harbour,** to which all declivities lead, is a little basin, three acres in extent and dry at low tide, protected by a double quay-head, between which is an entrance so narrow that it is barred against winter storms by horizontal baulks of timber dropped, one after another, into slots in the granite masonry. Outside, the narrow inlet leads obliquely to the open sea, between serrated crags only 50 yards apart.

From the western side of this channel the rocky ground rises sharply to '**Peak**', and thence to the summit of **Hard Head,** at 432 feet. On the seaward slopes of this hill are paths, seats and shelters, which render it a wonderful lounging-place for all, with superb views.

The crazy, lime-washed little cottages, many with outside stone staircases, constitute, with the towering wooded hillsides and the rocks, the chief glory of the place. At the side of the old Saxon Bridge, where the stream known as the *Rafiel* joins the head of the inner harbour, is the curious old **House on the Props,** now a restaurant.

The village is traversed by two main streets, which are interconnected at numerous points by little courts, alleys and lanes. The first comes over Sandy Hill by Killigarth and falls into Polperro with a gradient 'like the wall of a house'. It seems impossible that a mail coach ever came up (or went down) such an incline. It accompanies the stream to *Crumplehorn Mill,* perhaps half a mile up the valley, and then divides: one branch turning sharply to the left and running up a side valley towards Lansallos, the other climbing around the sides of the eastern hill

Polperro Harbour

for Pelynt and Looe. The second is one which leaves the Lansallos road at a point some 1½ miles out and descends into Polperro, at a somewhat break-neck pace, by another fold of the hills; runs through the village parallel to the first and terminates on the Fish Quay by the *Three Pilchards.*

Such, then, is Polperro: a human bees' hive stowed away in a cranny of the rocks. Its industries are four: the catching of fish, the painting of pictures, handicrafts and, above all, the entertainment of visitors. Until recently the village was solely a fishing community with a good sprinkling of artists. Of late years, in addition to a large increase in its artistic and literary circles, it has begun to experience some of the less desirable concomitants of fame.

Of unfailing interest to visitors is the **Smuggling Museum** (*April to mid-October, weekdays 10–7, Sunday 1–6.30; charge*) in Talland Street close to the harbour.

The road running eastward from Polperro climbs steeply and then drops to the beach at **Talland Bay** (*Talland Bay*). The sand is largely in evidence at low water, but the bay is one of great beauty and grandeur. It has been the scene of many wrecks, and although the bathing is good in places great care should be exercised, especially in diving from rocks, as there have been several fatalities.

A steep hills leads to **Talland Church,** the mother church of West Looe. The older parts of the building—the west wall, east window and tower—are attributed to the thirteenth century. The rest of the church dates from the late fifteenth or early sixteenth century. The fine wagon roof in the aisle and the bench-ends display good carving. Talland is one of six Cornish churches that have a tower separate from the main fabric. It is reached from the church by an arcade or long porch, covering a flight of rock steps. In this porch are preserved the old stocks and there is a good wagon roof. Among the monuments in the church are a fine carved slate tomb to John Bevyll (died 1578) and the sepulchral slab of 'Jone Mellow and her little sonne'.

The road continues past Portloe to—

Looe

Bathing Good and safe, from sand or rocks. Beach tents may be hired.

Boating Rowing, sailing and motor boats may be hired. There are daily cruises to

Polperro and Fowey.
Bowls Hannafore sea front.
Buses Services to Liskeard, Torpoint,
Plymouth and Polperro.
Distances Bodmin, 19 miles; Fowey, 24
(by ferry 10); Liskeard, 9; London, 228;
Plymouth, 20.
Early Closing Thursday.

Golf *Looe Bin Down Golf Club* off the
Looe–Torpoint road.
Hotels *Hannafore Point*, *Klymiarven*,
Looe, *Portbyhan*, *Rock Towers*.
Library Sea Front Court, East Looe.
Population 4,060.
Tennis At Hannafore.

The towns of East and West Looe are built on opposite sides of a deep
river valley. They form an ancient township and, beyond, the waterway
widens to lake-like proportions and in two streams wanders inland
between high hills for nearly 3 miles.

The Looes are of nearly equal antiquity, but West Looe is of considerably less commercial importance than its fellow. A picturesque granite
Bridge of seven main arches crosses the Harbour and connects the two
towns, incidentally providing a superb view.

The **Old Guildhall** of East Looe is now a museum (*April to Sep-*

Boats in the harbour at East Looe

tember, Monday to Friday 10–6, Sunday afternoons). Stone stairs and a wooden balustrade lead up to the large room where the free burgesses of East Looe formerly deliberated and where may be seen the ancient stocks. High up under the porch roof is the pillory. Between the Old Guildhall and the bridge is the modern **Guildhall** with clock tower. At Quay Head there is an interesting marine aquarium, the exhibits including sharks caught in Looe waters.

In Fore Street close by may be seen one of Looe's many charming examples of the domestic architecture of past centuries. This house, now a café, was for many years the residence of Thomas Bond (1765–1837), the historian of Looe and for nearly forty years Town Clerk of both East and West Looe. It contains a fine panelled room and other interesting pieces of antique house decoration: over a fireplace is the date 1652.

At **Church End,** the seaward extremity of East Looe, is Looe **Parish Church,** standing upon the site of a chapel dedicated to St Mary in the year 1259. Beyond the Church is a car park, and beyond that the **Promenade,** overlooking a sandy beach, the most popular bathing-place. To the right the stone **Pier,** known from its shape as 'The Banjo', forms the eastern arm of the Harbour entrance and provides an agreeable lounge and look-out.

West Looe also has plenty of interest, particularly the curious little quayside church of **St Nicholas.** The exact date of erection is unknown, but when its endowment was confirmed in 1336, upon the prayer of Sir John Dawney, it was referred to as having been built by the ancestors of that knight. It later served as Council chamber, Guildhall and Justice Room, until restored to ecclesiastical use in 1852. It then underwent considerable alteration and improvement. Reference must be made to the sunken vestry and the chancel rafters, made from timbers of the Spanish ship *San Josef,* captured by Nelson at the Battle of St Vincent.

From the church a picturesque cliff road, affording charming views, runs around the hill to **Hannafore,** a pleasant residential area facing the open sea. Those who know only Looe in the valley will be surprised at this attractive modern suburb with its extensive views over the sea and along the coast. At low tide the rocky foreshore is a grand place for juvenile crab-hunters and shrimpers. A ferry from Church End obviates the necessity of walking through both towns *via* the Bridge to reach Hannafore from East Looe.

The **Harbour,** as far as the bridge, often presents a busy scene. Here are seen numerous large fishing-luggers, for Looe is one of the principal fishing ports of Cornwall, and these little craft, with their tremendously long lines, their drift-nets or trawls, are to visitors a source of unlimited interest.

Looe Island lies half a mile south of Hannafore Point. It is about ¾ of a mile in circumference and about 150 feet high. A chapel and a three-gun battery stood upon the hill, but both have disappeared.

History In the roll of Edward III's fleet before Calais the port of Looe is said to have sent 20 ships and 315 sailors—only 5 ships fewer than London. Long before the reign of Queen Bess, Looe possessed a Mayor and free burgesses, and a charter granted in Armada year made 'nine of the more honest' chief burgesses. For centuries prior to 1832 East and West Looe each returned two Members to Parliament. The Corporation records go back 500 years. West Looe was incorporated by a charter of Queen Elizabeth in 1574, but the Corporation became extinct in 1869. The East Looe Corporation met for the last time in 1886.

Excursions from Looe

I. To Morval, Duloe and St Keyne

Follow the A387 beside the East Looe River to **Sandplace** and continue eastwards for about a mile to **Morval.** Close to the fine Elizabethan Morval House is the Church of St Wenna which dates mainly from the fifteenth century with Tudor and later additions. The walls have suffered severely from the weight of the wagon roof. Beautiful woodland stretches to the south while the summit of Tregarland Tor to the north gives entrancing views of the East Looe valley.

Return to Sandplace and turn right along the B3254 which leads through a beautiful wooded glen to **St Cuby's Well** on the left, bowered beneath a large leaning bay tree. Continue to **Duloe** where the church is a spacious Early English building noteworthy for its massive thirteenth-century tower of a type unusual in Cornwall, with buttresses and a pyramidal roof added when the church was restored in 1860. Fine monuments in the Colshull Chapel include that to Sir John Colshull (died 1483) depicting the knight in armour. A parclose screen of black oak encloses the chapel.

About 200 yards farther down the main road is a turning which at once brings into view a **Stone Circle** of quartz, of which seven stones remain upright and one lies prone.

The main road continues northward from Duloe to **St Keyne** known for its **Holy Well** ½ mile to the south-east. The husband or wife who is the first to drink of its waters is said to be sure of being the dominant partner. Few couples test the well's efficacy since the source has failed and the water is stagnant.

At **Paul Corin's Musical Collection** (*May to September, daily 10.30–1, 2.30–5; October to April, Sunday 2.30–5; charge*) demonstrations are given of the various mechanical organs housed in a most attractive hall.

II. To Seaton Valley and St Martin

The River Seaton rises inland on the moors and flows into the sea about 3 miles east of Looe. It is worth taking the coast road from East Looe notwithstanding its initial roughness. In 2 miles we come to Murrayton, the site of the **Woolly Monkey Sanctuary** (*Easter to September, daily 10.30–5.30; charge*). Visitors can watch, hear about and even meet the rare Amazon woolly monkeys which are bred there.

Continue to **Seaton** but do not cross the bridge at the river mouth, instead turn left along the B3247 which follows the river for nearly 3 miles to **Hessenford,** beautifully situated at the intersection of valleys between woods and grassy downs.

Turn left along the A387 and in 1 mile branch left along the B3253 which leads in 2 miles to **St Martin.** The church, which was until 1845 the parish church of East Looe, retains its Norman north doorway and original wagon roofs. In the aisle, notice the parclose screen erected in 1612 by Langdon of Keverell and ornamented with carved work, including some quaint and naïve mottoes. In the second pier of the arcade is a squint cut to enable the Squire of Keverell to see the preacher. In the south-east corner is an ambitious marble monument, with kneeling effigies, to Walter, the last of the Langdons and his wife (1676).

Seen in the chancel is an interesting incised slate slab displaying the likeness of Philip Maiowe, 1590. Note also a fine old carved chair; a few Jacobean carved bench-ends in the aisle, and the font constructed from parts of three different fonts, including the original Norman one.

Looe lies 1 mile to the south.

III. To Liskeard

Leave Looe by the A387 and in 2 miles branch left along the B3254 to reach—

Liskeard

Distances Bodmin, 13 miles; London, 222; Plymouth 17; St Austell, 20.
Early Closing Wednesday.
Hotel *Webbs.*

Library Barras Street.
Population 5,360.
Sports Sports complex at Lux Park.

Liskeard, 9 miles north of Looe, is an ancient municipal borough and market town noteworthy for its cattle fairs held on the second Monday of each month. The great annual Fair of St Matthew takes place on 2 October.

Though Liskeard is not a holiday resort, many motorists and others passing through are tempted by its attractive appearance to interrupt their journey; and the town is the centre for several interesting short excursions.

The **Church** is very fine and second largest in the county. The granite tower, 85 feet in height, was completed in 1903. There are 'leper' windows at the west end, by the tower, and some fine stained-glass windows.

Adjoining the Library is **Stuart House,** where in 1644 Charles I slept for seven nights. There are other ancient and noteworthy buildings in the town.

In Well Lane is the old **Pipe Well,** an interesting and unusual specimen dating originally from the late sixteenth century. Four pipes issue from an arched grotto and produce a never-failing supply of water.

Excursions from Liskeard

To St Cleer and the Cheesewring

Leave Liskeard by the B3254 Launceston road and in 1 mile keep left for **St Cleer.** The three-stage tower of the church rises 99 feet high. Within the church, features of interest include the Norman work in the north doorway, the thirteenth-century font, the stocks and a quaint seventeenth-century slate slab on the tomb of Robert Langeford.

Not far from the church, beside the road that passes its east gate, stands the famous **St Cleer's Well** dating from the fifteenth century. The baptistery over the well had been allowed to tumble to pieces, but it has been carefully restored with the original stones. The special merit of St Cleer was supposed to be its ability to cure madness.

About 1 mile north-east of St Cleer is **Trethevy Quoit,** a massive megalithic chamber 7 feet long and 9 feet high. One of the uprights supporting the huge capstone has fallen inward.

The Great Hall, Cotehele House, near Liskeard

Between St Cleer and Redgate Farm is the **Doniert Stone** with early interlacing designs and an inscription suggesting it may be connected with King Durngarth of Cornwall who died in 875. The scenery in this area is extremely wild, with huge boulders of granite protruding through the earth and numerous deserted mines with decayed and falling chimney shafts and buildings.

About 2½ miles north of St Cleer on the Upton Cross road is **Minions Mound,** said to be the burial place of a king. Nearby are **The Hurlers,** remains of three large Bronze Age circles. The great stones, according to legend, represent players of the Cornish game of hurling, who, for playing on Sundays, were turned into stone.

Continuing by a moorland track towards the rocky tor which rises out of the heath, after a tough climb over great granite boulders, we reach the wonderful pile of stones, each weighing many tons, called **The Cheesewring.** The balance of the huge stones is remarkable, though in modern times another pile has been built up under the top stone in case of need. From the hillcrest above The Cheesewring (1,250 feet) wonderful prospects over at least half of Cornwall may be enjoyed.

To St Ive and Callington

Leave Liskeard by the A390 Tavistock road which leads in 3 miles to **St Ive** (pronounced St Eve). Granite predominates in all parts of the fine church of the Decorated period. Note the unusually fine wagon roofs, the hagioscope and sedilia; the brightly tinctured Royal Arms of Charles II, dated 1660 and of heroic proportions; the parish stocks, and the sundial over the south porch inscribed 'Quotidie morior 1695.' Finest of all is the east window with its beautifully wrought stained glass and graceful niches on its sides. The tower, with its quartet of triple pinnacles is also impressive.

The church of **Quethiock,** 2 miles south of St Ive, is worth a detour. It has an unusual tower which apparently rises chimney-wise out of a roof end instead of seeming to stand on a separate base. The church has fine wagon roofs, rood-loft stairs and a large hagioscope, and the stocks are to be seen in the porch. In the floor is a brass of 1471 to Roger Kyngdon, his wife and sixteen children. There is a large cross in the churchyard, possibly dating from the thirteen century.

At **Newbridge,** 2 miles beyond St Ive the main road crosses the River Lynher by an angularly-recessed bridge, set in a scene of great rustic beauty. To the south looms the almost conical height of **Cadson Bury,** its brow encircled by a tremendous earthwork.

In a further 2 miles we reach **Callington,** which was once a parliamentary borough returning two members. It seems never to have had a corporation, being governed by a Portreeve and Reeve elected, with other officials, at the Court Leet of the manor of Kelly-Land.

It is an article of popular belief that King Arthur kept his court here in the sixth century, the place being then called Killiwick. In the Domesday Book it is registered as one of the King's towns, under the name of Calweton. In 1267 it received a market charter from Henry III.

The **Parish Church of St Mary,** an imposing granite edifice, was rebuilt in 1438 by Nicholas Assheton, one of the King's Judges, who, habited in the judicial costume of the period, is portrayed with his wife in a brass on the chancel floor.

This is one of the few Cornish churches that have anything in the nature of a clerestory: there are three little windows on the south side of the nave and four on the north. The roof and double arcade seem to indicate that the north aisle was added to the church in a somewhat unusual fashion.

On the north side of the chancel is the alabaster tomb, with life-size effigy of the first Lord Willoughby de Broke (died 1502), who was Steward of the Duchy of Cornwall, Lord of Kelly-Land, and patron of this living. His armour is a fine suit of plate, the mail hauberk showing at neck and thigh. At his left knee is the Garter, and he wears also the Mantle, Collar and George of that Order. At his feet are two small figures of friars. Although defaced, this is a fine monument.

Leave Callington by the Tavistock road and at the first cross-roads turn right to reach **Dupath Well.** Architecturally this is the most important of all Cornish holy wells because whereas in most cases there is little more than a tiny arch or vault over a cistern sunk in some bank or hillside, here we have a distinct chapel, or baptistery, probably dating from the fifteenth century, with doorway and window mullion of dressed stone. The walls are of roughly squared granite blocks, one more than 11 feet long extending the length of the east wall.

The high point 1½ miles north-east of Callington, is **Kit Hill.** On the summit (1,091 feet), is a tall mine chimney.

Nearby, at **Calstock** is the fine medieval Cotehele House (*April to October, open daily ; November to March gardens only ; charge*).

To St Neot

Follow the A38 Bodmin road for 4 miles to Two Waters Foot and then turn right to follow the St Neot River to the village of **St Neot.** The church has a magnificent series of late fifteenth- and early sixteenth-century stained-glass windows, famous throughout the West of England. They are quite beyond any possibility of rivalry in Cornwall—a county not rich in this class of ecclesiastical ornament—and as an aggregation of early glass can have few equals elsewhere. Some of the features are unique. In 1937–9 the windows which had been restored in 1825 by J. P. Hedgeland were carefully repaired. The subjects are as follows (beginning at the east chancel window and travelling round the church clockwise):

(1) The Creation Window.
(2) The Noah Window.
(3) The Borlase window.
(4) The Martyn window.
(5) The Mutton window.
(6) The Calway window.
(7) The Tubbe and Calway window.
(8) Armorial window (Hedgeland).
(9) St George window.
(10) The St Neot's window (showing in twelve designs the legendary history of the saint).
(11) The Young Women's window.
(12) The Wives' window.
(13) The Harys window.
(14) The Redemption window (Hedgeland).
(15) The Acts window.
(16) The Chancel window (The Last Supper by Hedgeland).

Note also the fine barrel-roofed porch with upper chamber, the font and the massive tower, and the richly carved pinnacles of tower, porch and roof.

On the north side of the chancel is the desecrated tomb of the saint. For a time his remains lay in peace within the sarcophagus; but the wave of relic-worship reached even to this secluded hamlet, and the venerated skeleton was removed entire (save for one arm) to the Benedictine Monastery in Huntingdonshire which afterwards gave the name of St Neots to a neighbouring town.

The churchyard has five ancient crosses, including the decapitated one which is regarded as 'St Neot's,' and has a well-ornamented shaft. The head of a cross recently discovered in the churchyard is thought to be the missing one.

IV. To Rame Head, Antony and St Germans

From Seaton (see page 149) the B3247 runs eastward close to the coast. It soon reaches the select resort of Downderry (*Sea View, Wide Sea*) and continues over the downs to Portwrinkle (*Whitsand Bay*). The village, reached by a steep lane, has a small harbour with a pier and there are two sheltered beaches providing safe bathing. The old pilchard cellar dating from the fifteenth century should be visited. There is a golf course to the north and on it, to the left of the Crafthole road, is a dovecot erected by the Dawnay family in the fourteenth century.

At the straggling village of Crafthole a left turn leads to **Sheviock,** a typical English wayside village on the A374. The church has a remarkable broach spire over a thirteenth-century tower, while the rest of the building dates mainly from the fourteenth and fifteenth centuries. The wagon roof in the north aisle, the carved bench-ends and the old stocks are noteworthy features. In the south transept under a restored canopy may be seen stone effigies of Sir Edward Courtenay (died 1370) and his wife.

Return to the main road, shortly forking right along the Millbrook road and then in ½ mile making a right turn on to the cliff road leading to Rame Head. Huts, tents and bungalows dot the hillside and a number of masked batteries will also be noticed, all of them obsolete. The village of **Rame** is interesting for the little church of St German which contains Norman work, notably one of the few tympana existing in Cornwall. It is of carved slate and is now mounted in the west wall of the nave. There is a fine wagon roof with carved ornamentation in the south aisle and some of the old bench-ends remain. The hagioscope and rood-loft stairs should also be noticed.

A short distance from the church rises the promontory of **Rame Head,** from which the cliffs descend sharply on either side. The **Chapel** at the point is perhaps 7 yards long and 3 yards wide inside, with walls upwards of a yard thick. It has a vaulted stone roof and presents an interesting appearance of antiquity. There are four windows and a doorway: the east window is of course the largest, but the framing and tracery are missing from all and the ancient oratory is little better than a ruin. This building is known to have been dedicated in 1397 and 1425 to St Michael and is thought to have provided (with at least two other chapels) a series of guiding points to the entrance of Sutton Pool, in effect a medieval lighthouse.

Penlee Point to the east offers little of interest other than the fog-horn station and it is best to retrace one's steps for Rame, bearing right to **Cawsand** and **Kingsand** which offer beautiful views across Plymouth Sound and a maze of narrow streets, tortuous alleys and irregularly built cottages so characteristic of Cornish villages. Take the road north-east out of Kingsand to join the B3247 near **Maker Heights** which again offer a fine panorama of the Plymouth area.

Shortly on the right is the entrance to **Mount Edgcumbe** (*house and higher gardens, May to September, Monday and Tuesday 2–6, charge; park and lower gardens, all year, daily, free*). The sixteenth-century house was burnt out during the Second World War though much has been restored. The fine gardens and deer park offer outstanding coastal views.

Return along the B3247 to the large village of **Millbrook** which stands at the head of a wide but shallow creek. Bear to the right along the waterfront and to the left after passing All Saint's Church and follow the winding high-banked lane through leafy dells, by farmsteads and orchards, to the village of **St John** whose beauty has remained unspoilt by time. Mellow cottages stand behind high hedges in luxuriant gardens; farmyards abut upon the road; in season apple-trees suspend their fragrant blossoms above the roadway. Beside a stream stands the squat Norman tower of the church.

Antony House, Torpoint

The same beautiful road leads in less than a mile to **Antony,** another old-world village though less quiet than St John since it stands on the main Torpoint road. The church contains some interesting monuments including a fine brass of 1420 to Margery Arundell. **Antony House** (*April to September, Tuesday, Wednesday and Thursday also Bank Holiday Mondays 2–6; charge*), owned by the National Trust, is one of the finest Queen Anne houses in the West Country. Built by Sir William Carew between 1711 and 1721, it contains collections of paintings, furniture, china and objets d'art.

The return may be made to Looe by the B3247. If the main A374 road is taken it is worth turning right at Polbathic to see the Norman church at **St Germans.** This was the cathedral of Cornwall in the Saxon era and it exhibits more Norman work than any other church in the county. Outstanding are the west front with two powerful buttressed towers and the first two bays on the south side of the nave.

Return to the main road and shortly fork left along the A387 to reach Hessenford from which the route is as in Excursion II.

Index

Where more than one reference is given, the first is the principal.

158